Collins

Enhanced English Alive Coursebook 5

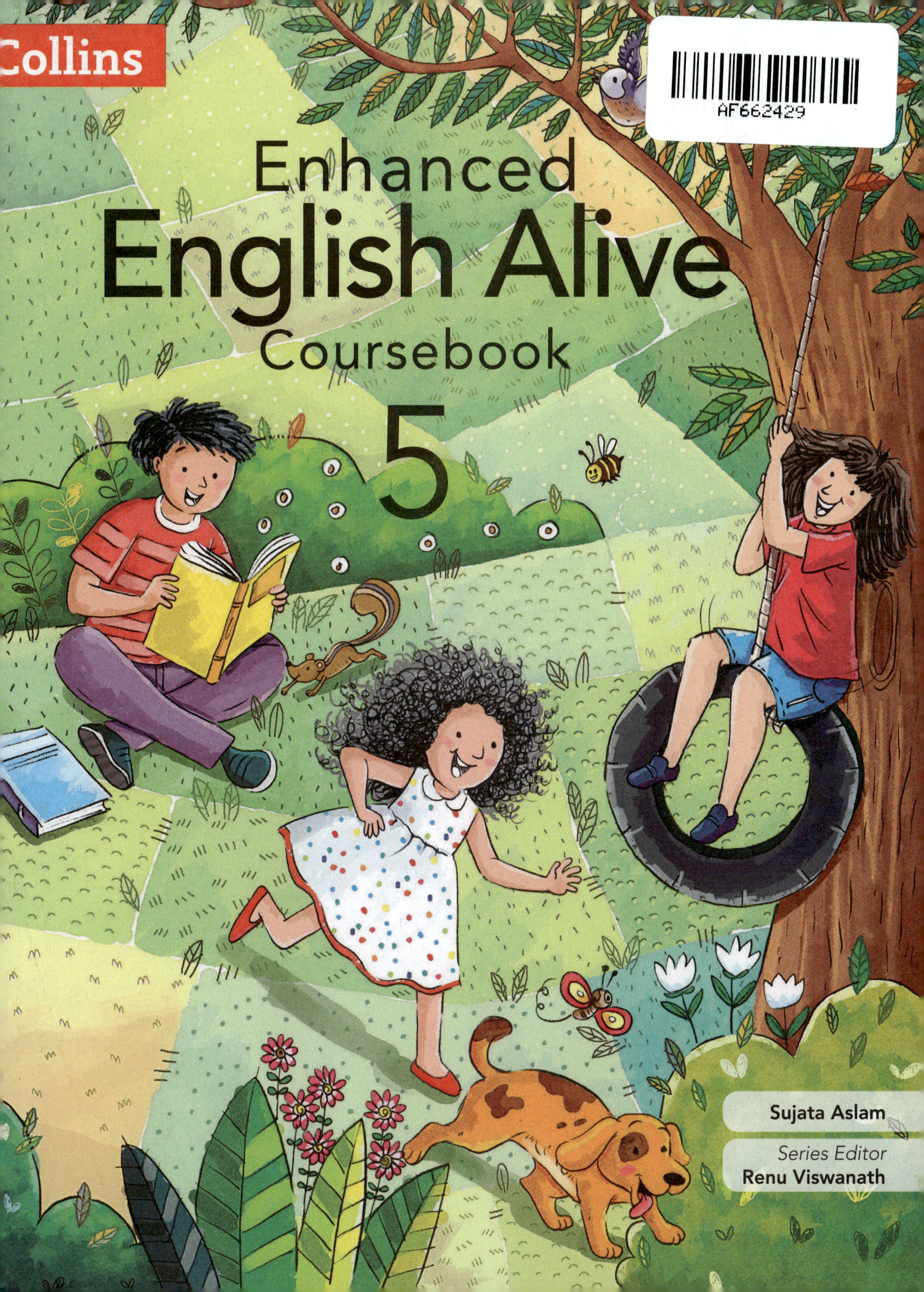

Sujata Aslam

Series Editor
Renu Viswanath

Acknowledgements

The publishers wish to thank and acknowledge the following for granting us permission to use copyright material:

Chuskit Goes to School, written by Sujatha Padmanabhan, published by Pratham Books (© Pratham Books, 2007) on StoryWeaver. The story is a collaborative initiative of NIPWD (Namgyal Institute for People with Disabilities) and Pratham Books.

The publishers have applied for permission for the following:
In Father's Presence by R. K. Narayan, *Trapped* by Sigrun Srivastav, *Underground* by James Reeves, *Awareness About Our Environment* by Sylvia Stults, *The Wizard of Oz* by L. Frank Baum (play adaptation), *Sailing Out to Space* by Gareth Lancaster.
Acknowledgements for these texts will be made in the future editions of the book.

Every effort has been made to trace copyright holders and to obtain their permission for the use of copyright material. However, in some instances, we have been unable to trace the owners of the copyright pieces published here. The authors and publishers will gladly receive any information enabling them to rectify any error or omission in subsequent editions.

Illustrations

Cover and Title Page: Created by Toonfantasy

Inside: Page 14: Santi Visalli Contributor; STR Stringer, Library of Congress; **26:** Kailash Kumar; **34:** triloks; **37:** Lisitsa; **38:** Graiki; **54:** Peter Cade; **66:** Instants; **67:** Jenny Dettrick, KarenHBlack, Yuki Angeline; **68:** David Trood; 77: petovarga, blueringmedia, colematt; **82:** OnBlast; **96:** Olga Naumova; **129:** orangemilky; **130:** bubble86, klyaksun, blueringmedia, Dmitry Mirolyubov, Lisitsa.

Preface

Enhanced English Alive is a multi-skill course in English that adheres to the guidelines laid down by the **National Education Policy, 2020**. This edition retains the original essence of teaching communicative English using a cross-curricular approach and interactive and experiential teaching and learning methods. It offers high-quality English language materials with a coherent structured approach, effective integration of subject knowledge and life skills.

The series comprises Coursebooks and Workbooks for Foundational Stage (Nursery, LKG, UKG, Classes 1 and 2), Preparatory Stage (Classes 3 to 5), and Middle Stage (Classes 6 to 8). Literature Readers are for the Preparatory and Middle Stages (Classes 3 to 8). Each grade package includes a Teacher's Resource Pack and a Collins DigiSuite.

This series integrates the essence of **NIPUN Bharat** guidelines, which extensively deal with foundational literacy and numeracy. Each book aims to motivate learners to read independently, to improve their vocabulary, to develop their critical thinking and creative skills, as well as to enhance their ability to express themselves both verbally and in writing.

This series takes care of the requirements of **Structured Assessments For Analyzing Learning (SAFAL)**. Research-based activities and projects have been used to instill inquiry-based learning, while comprehension passages have been followed by extrapolative and value-based questions that involve analysis-based learning. Additionally, in the Middle Stage (Classes 6 to 8), an end-of year question paper is provided which is based on the latest CBSE guidelines.

Key features

Coursebooks

- **Warm-up:** A wide variety of picture-based fun activities or probing questions at the beginning of chapters initiate the learner into the subject and ensure his/her active engagement in the lesson. For grades 1 to 5, these activities are introspective and meditative inquiries that are based on the pedagogy of mindfulness as delineated in the NEP, 2020.
- **Reading:** Each book has well-chosen selections from a wide range of literary genres that are also useful in cross-curricular teaching. These include picture stories and comic strips.
- **Cross-curricular boxes:** This series specially covers topics that are interrelated with other subjects taught in the same grade. Dedicated boxes teaching these cross-curricular concepts are placed along the main text.
- **Glossary:** All new words in the text are highlighted and their meanings are given in simple language using the easiest possible words. Literary devices are also taught along with a glossary of literary terms.
- **Summary:** A short summary at the end of each text is provided for an easy way to remember the essence of the text.
- **Comprehension:** This section includes plenty of exercises including factual, inferential, and extrapolative questions.
- **Life Skills and Values:** There is a separate thematic section on life skills and values aimed at developing good character in students and equipping them with skills needed to cope with

different challenges in life. Guidelines set by NEP, 2020 have been followed in selecting these life skills and values.

- **Vocabulary:** Each chapter has boxed explanations of new vocabulary words and topics followed by a variety of exercises. Spelling is also taught in this section with proper rules and explanations. Moreover, dictionary skills are taught in books 3 to 5.
- **Grammar:** Grade-appropriate grammar is explained with several visual models and extensive examples from the learner's immediate world. Plenty of varied exercises follow them to ensure the learner has learnt the concept well.
- **Listening and Speaking:** This section aims at developing students' listening, speaking, and overall communicative skills through a wide variety of tasks and pair/group activities. Pronunciation is also covered in this section in books 3 to 5.
- **Writing:** This well-graded section has a variety of age-appropriate creative and scaffolded writing tasks. These cover informal and formal letters, diary entries, flow charts, posters, stories, biographies, notices, reports, travelogues, character sketches, book reviews, recipes, acrostic poems, articles, and picture-based compositions.
- **Activities:** There is a fun activity accompanying each poem. Most of these activities require working collaboratively in groups or pairs. These activities are varied and cover various twenty-first century life skills.
- **Projects:** Three well-designed cross-curricular projects are provided that are linked to topics taught in that particular grade in other subjects.
- **Cross-curricular Vocabulary:** A word bank teaching cross-curricular vocabulary is included at the end of books 3 to 5. Words are classified according to different subjects and categories.

Workbooks

The Workbooks have been carefully mapped to the Coursebooks, and created with the intention of independent learning. Each Workbook has 8 comprehension passages including poems. The vocabulary and grammar sections include a quick recap of the concepts covered in the corresponding chapter of the Coursebook. The listening, speaking, and writing sections allow learners extra practice. Additional assessment papers included in the Workbooks are patterned on the Structured Assessments For Analyzing Learning (SAFAL). These offer a scope for assessing the competencies of critical thinking, inquiry-based learning, and analysis-based learning.

Literature Readers

The Literature Readers teach critical appreciation of literature through short stories, folktales, fairytales, poems and extracts from classics from the literature of different ages. A summary at the end offers a revision and understanding of the essence of the text. Literary devices are also taught along with a glossary of literary terms.

Teacher's Resource Pack

The Teacher's Resource Pack contains model lesson plans, additional worksheets, and grammar-based projects covering all the pedagogical aspects included in the Coursebooks, along with listening texts and answer keys to all exercises across Coursebooks, Workbooks, Literature Readers, and additional assessment papers.

Key to Icons

Enhanced English Alive is a multi-skill course that is closely aligned with the National Education Policy, 2020. It uses an interactive approach, cross-curricular themes, and experiential activities to build communicative competence in students. This series aims to prepare learners with the various skills outlined in the National Education Policy, 2020. These skills have been tagged appropriately with easily recognizable icons for the user's convenience. Here is the key to all the icons used in this series.

Cross-Curricular Content

- The cross-curricular approach to a topic recognizes that all subjects are interlinked. It includes contributions from several different disciplines or viewpoints for effective learning.
- All chapters have dedicated boxes teaching cross-curricular content appropriate to that class. These boxes cover the following:
  - ***Science Scan*** covers topics related to science.
  - ***Maths Magic*** covers topics related to mathematics.
  - ***Earth Speak*** covers topics related to geography and environmental studies.
  - ***Looking Back*** covers topics related to historical events and personalities.
  - ***Fact File*** covers topics related to general knowledge and awareness.
  - ***Lit Bits*** covers topics related to literature and famous literary figures.
  - ***Art and Culture*** covers topics related to art and culture.

Twenty-First Century Skills

- The twenty-first century skills ensure that today's students can thrive in an ever-changing world and can use these skills to learn constantly.
- Here are the most commonly cited twenty-first century skills in this series:

Critical Thinking

Communication Skills

Collaboration

Creativity

Information Communication Technology Skills or Digital Literacy

Experiential Learning

- Experiential learning is a process of learning through hands-on experience. Here, students 'learn by doing' an activity followed by reflective observation on the experience from multiple perspectives.
- This method helps learners link existing knowledge to understand new concepts and apply it to make decisions.

Art Integration

- Art Integrated Learning (AIL) is a teaching-learning model that integrates fine arts (painting, sculpture, architecture, music, and poetry), performing arts (theatre and dance), and photography with teaching new concepts.
- This provides students with an experiential and a multi-disciplinary learning experience.

Happiness Content

- Learning should be an enjoyable process for learners. It should focus on building and understanding new concepts rather than rote learning.
- Children should experience happiness through learning and awareness, active participation in class, and also in their relationships with their friends and family.

India Focus

- India Focus puts spotlight on the heritage, culture, customs, and history and geography of the Indian subcontinent.
- This provides students a deeper understanding of their homeland and creates a sense of solidarity.

Sustainable Development Goals

- The Sustainable Development Goals, adopted by the United Nations in 2015, are a collection of 17 interlinked global goals designed to achieve a better and more sustainable future for all by 2030. Here are the 17 goals:

Key Features

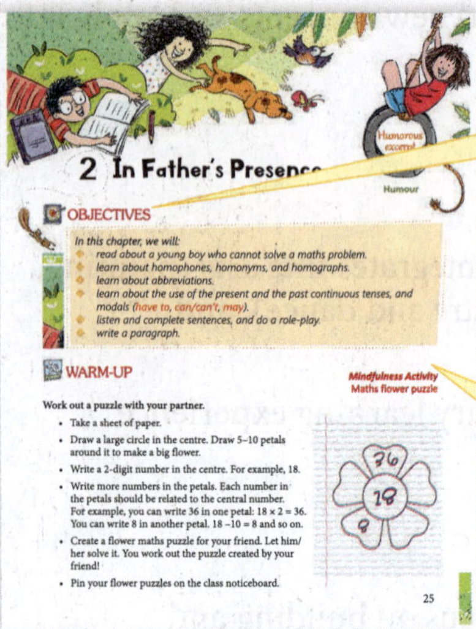

2 In Father's Presence

Humour

OBJECTIVES

In this chapter, we will:
- read about a young boy who cannot solve a maths problem.
- learn about homophones, homonyms, and homographs.
- learn about abbreviations.
- learn about the use of the present and the past continuous tenses, and modals (have to, can/can't, may).
- listen and complete sentences, and do a role-play.
- write a paragraph.

WARM-UP

Mindfulness Activity
Maths flower puzzle

Work out a puzzle with your partner.
- Take a sheet of paper.
- Draw a large circle in the centre. Draw 5–10 petals around it to make a big flower.
- Write a 2-digit number in the centre. For example, 18.
- Write more numbers in the petals. Each number in the petals should be related to the central number. For example, you can write 36 in one petal: 18 × 2 = 36. You can write 8 in another petal. 18 − 10 = 8 and so on.
- Create a flower maths puzzle for your friend. Let him/her solve it. You work out the puzzle created by your friend!
- Pin your flower puzzles on the class noticeboard.

25

Page 25

Objectives: All learning goals for the chapter listed out

Warm-up: Mindfulness activities to help train the student's mind to be involved in the present moment without getting distracted, followed by theme-based warm-ups

Comprehension: Covers factual, inferential, and extrapolative questions

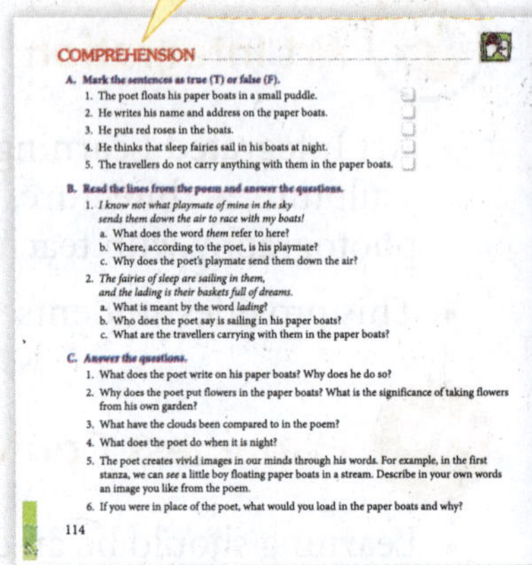

COMPREHENSION

A. Mark the sentences as true (T) or false (F).
1. The poet floats his paper boats in a small puddle.
2. He writes his name and address on the paper boats.
3. He puts red roses in the boats.
4. He thinks that sleep fairies sail in his boats at night.
5. The travellers do not carry anything with them in the paper boats.

B. Read the lines from the poem and answer the questions.
1. I know not what playmate of mine in the sky sends them down the air to race with my boats!
   a. What does the word them refer to here?
   b. Where, according to the poet, is his playmate?
   c. Why does the poet's playmate send them down the air?
2. The fairies of sleep are sailing in them, and the lading is their baskets full of dreams.
   a. What is meant by the word lading?
   b. Who does the poet say is sailing in his paper boats?
   c. What are the travellers carrying with them in the paper boats?

C. Answer the questions.
1. What does the poet write on his paper boats? Why does he do so?
2. Why does the poet put flowers in the paper boats? What is the significance of taking flowers from his own garden?
3. What have the clouds been compared to in the poem?
4. What does the poet do when it is night?
5. The poet creates vivid images in our minds through his words. For example, in the first stanza, we can see a little boy floating paper boats in a stream. Describe in your own words an image you like from the poem.
6. If you were in place of the poet, what would you load in the paper boats and why?

114

Page 114

Life Skills and Values: Value-based questions to develop good character through experiential learning

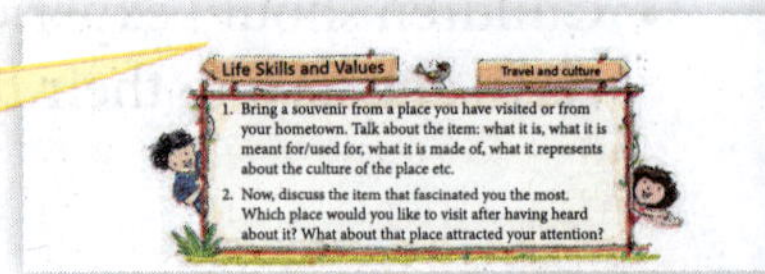

Life Skills and Values — Travel and culture

1. Bring a souvenir from a place you have visited or from your hometown. Talk about the item: what it is, what it is meant for/used for, what it is made of, what it represents about the culture of the place etc.
2. Now, discuss the item that fascinated you the most. Which place would you like to visit after having heard about it? What about that place attracted your attention?

Page 115

Reading: A good balance of Indian and global selections from a wide range of literary genres that are useful in cross-curricular teaching

Cross-curricular boxes: Topics related to other subjects highlighted

Glossary: Meanings for new words and literary devices given alongside the text

READING

Have you ever dreamt of travelling to space? What would you do in space? Read this poem by Gareth Lancaster to find out what the poet wants to do there.

I dream of sailing out to space[1],
Upon a yacht of stars.
With port holes all along the sides,
I'd gaze amazed at Mars.

With mast made strong with spider[2] webs,
And sail of fluffy cloud,
I'd watch the Earth go sweeping past,
As out to space I ploughed.

With stars in front and stars behind,
And planets far and near,
I'd sail my yacht around the rings,
Of Saturn with a cheer.

Science Scan
- Saturn is the second-largest planet in the solar system, but it is very light for its size.
- Saturn has beautiful rings around it, made of billions of tiny chips of ice and dust.

Literary Device
1. and 2. The consonant s has been repeated in sailing out to space and strong with spider webs. Such a repetition of a sound is called alliteration.

yacht (pronounced yawt): a large sailing boat, often with an engine and a place to sleep on, used for pleasure trips and racing
port holes: small, circular windows on the outside of a ship
amazed: very surprised
made strong: (here) tied together
fluffy: soft and light
ploughed: moved through something
cheer: happiness

142

Page 142

Vocabulary: Covers language skills with focus on usage

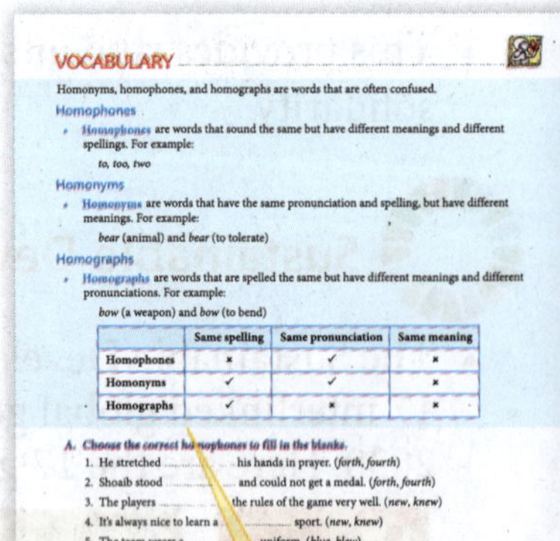

VOCABULARY

Homonyms, homophones, and homographs are words that are often confused.

Homophones
- Homophones are words that sound the same but have different meanings and different spellings. For example:
  to, too, two

Homonyms
- Homonyms are words that have the same pronunciation and spelling, but have different meanings. For example:
  bear (animal) and bear (to tolerate)

Homographs
- Homographs are words that are spelled the same but have different meanings and different pronunciations. For example:
  bow (a weapon) and bow (to bend)

	Same spelling	Same pronunciation	Same meaning
Homophones	×	✓	×
Homonyms	✓	✓	×
Homographs	✓	×	×

A. Choose the correct homophones to fill in the blanks.
1. He stretched ______ his hands in prayer. (forth, fourth)
2. Shoaib stood ______ and could not get a medal. (forth, fourth)
3. The players ______ the rules of the game very well. (new, knew)
4. It's always nice to learn a ______ sport. (new, knew)
5. The team wears a ______ uniform. (blue, blew)

Page 3

Summary: A short summary at the end of each text for a mental revision and an easier way of remembering the essence of the text

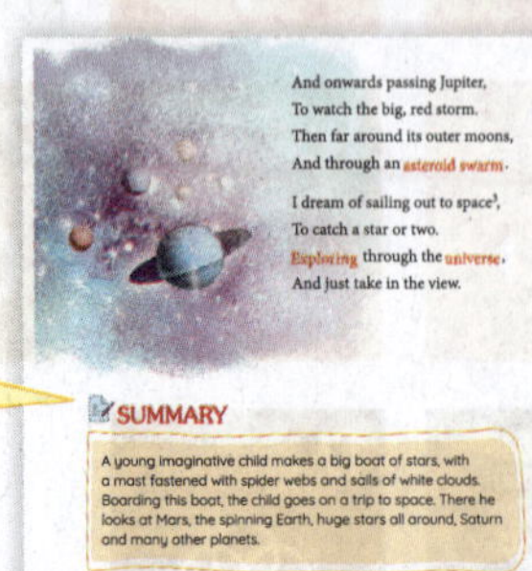

And onwards passing Jupiter,
To watch the big, red storm.
Then far around its outer moons,
And through an asteroid swarm.

I dream of sailing out to space[1],
To catch a star or two.
Exploring through the universe,
And just take in the view.

SUMMARY

A young imaginative child makes a big boat of stars, with a mast fastened with spider webs and sails of white clouds. Boarding this boat, the child goes on a trip to space. There he looks at Mars, the spinning Earth, huge stars all around, Saturn and many other planets.

Page 143

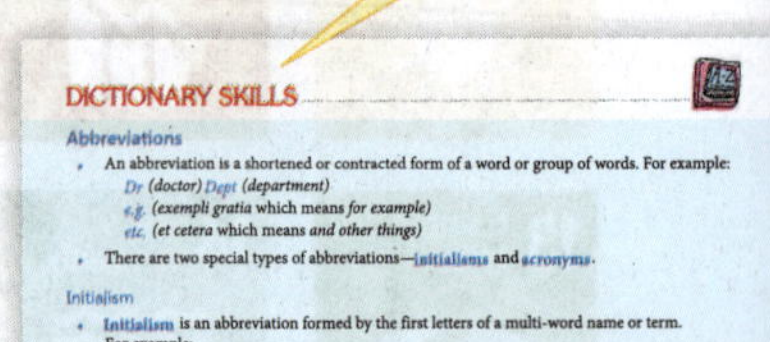

DICTIONARY SKILLS

Abbreviations
- An abbreviation is a shortened or contracted form of a word or group of words. For example:
  Dr (doctor) Dept (department)
  e.g. (exempli gratia which means for example)
  etc. (et cetera which means and other things)
- There are two special types of abbreviations—initialisms and acronyms.

Initialism
- Initialism is an abbreviation formed by the first letters of a multi-word name or term. For example:

Page 3

Grammar: Grade-appropriate grammar explained with several visual models and extensive examples, followed by exercises

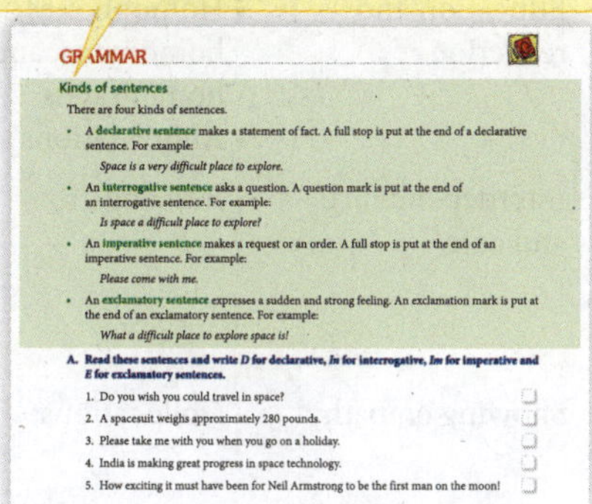

Page 137

Writing: A well-graded section with a variety of creative and scaffolded writing tasks:

- letter writing
- diary entry
- flow charts
- poster making
- biography
- notice writing
- report-writing
- travelogue writing
- character sketch
- book review
- recipe writing
- acrostic poem
- data interpretation
- picture composition

Activity: A collaborative fun activity with each poem

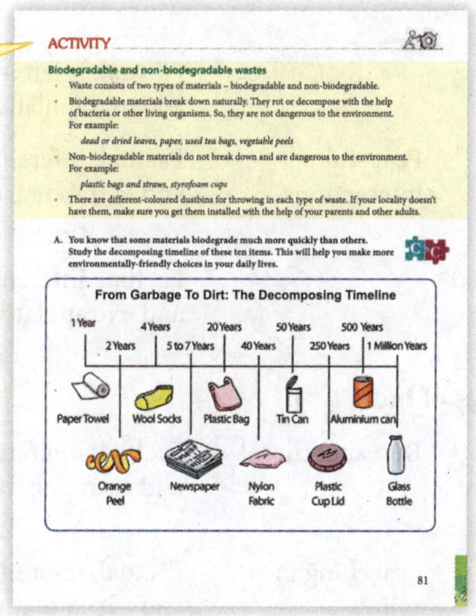

Page 81

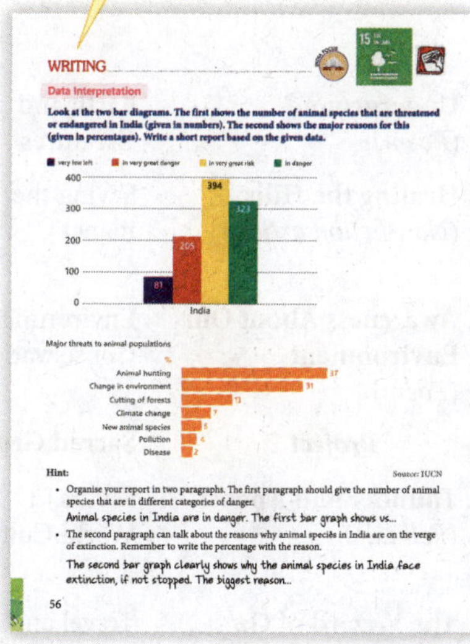

Page 56

Listening and Speaking: A wide variety of communicative activities leading to collaboration and team building; also covers pronunciation

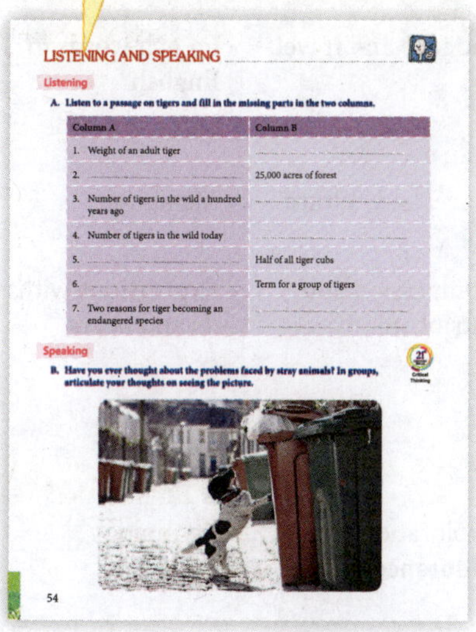

Page 54

Project: Three cross-curricular projects linked to topics taught in other subjects in this grade

Page 83

This series integrates the essence of ***NIPUN Bharat*** *guidelines and the requirements of* ***Structured Assessments For Analyzing Learning (SAFAL).***

Detailed Contents

Grammar	Listening and Speaking	Writing/Activity
• Abstract nouns • Forming abstract nouns • Subject-verb agreement	• Listening to a passage on Eklavya and marking T/F • Role-playing a situation on being considerate • *t* pronounced as *ch*	• Writing an email
• Present continuous tense • Past continuous tense • Modals: *have to, can/can't, may*	• Listening to a passage about Vedic Maths and filling in the blanks • Role-playing a situation on counselling a friend	• Writing a paragraph
		• Group initiatives for community
• Degrees of comparison • *will* and *going to* for future time	• Listening to a passage on tigers and filling in the missing information in a column • Picture analysis on the problems faced by stray animals and providing solutions • Syllables	• Data interpretation
		• Creating and playing an animal quiz • Treating animals the right way
• Adjectives ending in *-ing* and *-ed* • Adverbs	• Listening to a passage about an Indian environmentalist and filling in a form • Role-playing a situation between a parent and a child	• Writing an article • Writing an acrostic poem
		• Studying a decomposing timeline • Sorting biodegradable and non-biodegradable wastes
• Subject-verb-object structure • *for* and *since*	• Listening to a conversation and filling in the blanks • Sharing one's thoughts on reusing everyday items • Silent letters *b, l, r* and *s*	• Describing a procedure
• Direct and reported speech • Reporting verbs • Inverted commas	• Listening to a description and filling in the blanks • Creating and presenting a mind map on how to reduce the impact of natural disasters • Pronunciation of *ch*	• Creating a comic strip
		• Making dolls representing different countries
• Active and passive voice • *whose* and *which*	• Listening to descriptions of animals and completing a table • Role-playing an interview with a character from the story • Silent letters *g, k, n* and *w*	• Writing a travelogue
• Kinds of sentences • Transformation of sentences • *if* clauses	• Listening to a story and numbering events in order • Enacting a skit or describing a lunar eclipse	• Writing a story based on pictures
		• Making a chart or scrapbook on *A Colony on Mars*

Contents

1 Chuskit Goes to School

Helping the Community

OBJECTIVES

In this chapter, we will:

- *read a heart-warming story of a girl who cannot walk.*
- *learn about compound adjectives.*
- *learn to arrange words in alphabetical order.*
- *learn about abstract nouns and subject-verb agreement.*
- *listen to a story and answer questions.*
- *role-play a situation.*
- *write an email.*

WARM-UP

Mindfulness Activity
Sharing abilities

A. All of us are different from each other in terms of our abilities. Let's play a game in pairs. Choose a partner. Remember, roles are going to be reversed for each step.

1. Blindfold your partner. Hold their hand and get them to walk around the classroom, corridor, or school garden. Let them describe their feelings as they walk blindfolded.
2. Think of the names of three books/films. Enact the names through gestures and ask your partner to guess the titles.
3. Request your partner to hop on one leg. Ask them to talk about how it feels when they are not using both their legs.

B. Match the pictures with the descriptions of these differently-abled people.

1. 

2. 

3. 

a. **Helen Keller**, an American author, was the first deaf and blind person to go to college. She proved to the world that deaf and blind people could also learn to communicate and lead a successful life.

b. **Stephen Hawking** was an English scientist and author of *A Brief History of Time*. He suffered from ALS, a disease that had gradually paralysed him over the years. He communicated using a speech-generating device.

c. **Sudha Chandran** is an Indian film and television actress. She lost a leg following a road accident. She, however, continued dancing, and went on to become a famous Bharatanatyam dancer.

INDIA FOCUS

5 GENDER EQUALITY

READING

Chuskit is a little girl who cannot go to school because she is unable to walk. Let's find out if her dream of going to school and receiving education comes true.

Chuskit woke up early that morning. It was a very special day and she was too excited to sleep till late. She eagerly looked out of the window next to her bed. It was spring time in Ladakh and the apricot trees were in full bloom. Ama-ley was awake too. Chuskit could hear Ama-ley in the kitchen making gur-gur tea. This was a day Chuskit was going to remember for a long time. Can you guess why? No, it was not Losar. That was many months away. Nor was it any other special day in her village, like the gonpa festival, or a wedding day.

Today was going to be Chuskit's first day at school. At nine years, she had waited a long, long time for this. The school was not very far away from her home. To get there, you had to walk up to the main road. Just before the prayer wheel, you took the path to the left of the road that ran along a narrow stream. Near the poplar trees, you crossed the stream by jumping over the big rocks.

eagerly: showing a lot of interest or excitement about something
Ama-ley: 'mother' in Ladakhi language
gur-gur tea: butter tea that is made in a long cylindrical wooden vessel. The tea is churned with butter, salt, and milk in this vessel. A low *gur-gur* noise is produced during churning.
Losar: a festival celebrating the Ladakhi or Tibetan New Year. It has its origin in the fifteenth century.
gonpa: a Buddhist monastery
prayer wheel: A prayer wheel is made of a hollow metal cylinder, and fixed on a handle. On the outside of the cylinder are prayers in Sanskrit. Buddhist devotees spin these wheels.

Once you got to the other side, a short walk up a slope took you to the school. All the children of Skitpo Yul, Chuskit's village, walked to school every day. But not little Chuskit. She could not walk.

Chuskit was born with legs that did not work like everyone else's. Her father had taken her to the village amchi and then to the doctors in Leh. But no amount of medicine had helped her walk. At first, Chuskit did not realise that she was in any way different from Stobdan, her younger brother, or her cousins. But soon there were many things she could not do as easily as they could.

'That does not matter,' her Aba-ley would tell her. 'You can stitch better than any of them. And you draw very well.' Aba-ley often brought her some colour pencils from Leh.

Chuskit used a chair fitted with wheels to move around. Elders called it a wheelchair. When Aba-ley first brought the wheelchair home, everyone in her family was very excited. 'Now I won't have to carry Chuskit everywhere. I can wheel her around,' said Ama-ley, with tears of happiness in her eyes. 'And I will be able to go wherever I want!' cried Chuskit excitedly.

Slowly, Chuskit learnt to use her wheelchair. She would ask her mother to seat her in the wheelchair outside her home every evening.

One evening, when Chuskit was sitting outside the house with her grandfather, a young boy came up to her. He carried a letter which he handed over to her grandfather. 'Julley! The bus driver asked me to give this to you,' he said.

'My name is Abdul,' he said turning to Chuskit. 'I study in Class 6 at the government school. I have often wondered why you don't come to school.'

'Julley, Abdul,' said Chuskit. 'I have never been to school. The path to the school is too uneven and pebbly and my wheelchair will get stuck. It would be very difficult for my parents to carry me to school and back every day.'

'But would you like to come to school?' asked Abdul.

'Of course!' replied Chuskit. 'I hear my younger brother talk of all the things he does at school. I want to study like everyone else,

Earth Speak

- Ladakh is a union territory. It is a high altitude, cold region in the Himalayas.
- It is bounded by the Karakarom and the Himalayan mountain ranges.
- Ladakh is thinly populated. Leh is the largest town there.

amchi: a doctor practising the Tibetan system of medicine, also called amchi
Aba-ley: 'father' in Ladakhi language
Julley: a greeting in Ladakhi language, meaning 'hello' and 'goodbye'

make friends, play games, wear a uniform and even write exams. You may not believe this, but I sometimes dream of carrying a school bag, even eating packed lunch...'

'Enough! Enough!' interrupted her grandfather. 'Stop dreaming, Chuskit. You know you cannot go to school.'

'Meme-ley, please,' pleaded Chuskit softly with tears in her eyes as her grandfather walked away angrily. 'Meme-ley does not understand how I feel,' said Chuskit. 'I too want to learn to read and do maths. Do you understand?'

'I do,' said Abdul. 'Chuskit, I will see you later. I must go now. Julley!'

The next day, Abdul went straight to the headmaster's room after assembly. 'Julley, Azhang-ley!' he said. 'I want to talk to you about a girl from our village who does not go to school. She is Stobdan's sister, Chuskit.'

'Oh yes,' replied the headmaster. 'I know her. She is unable to walk, isn't she?'

'Yes, Azhang-ley. She uses a wheelchair to move around but cannot reach school, as the path from her home is too rough and uneven. I was wondering if we could all get together and level the path and build a small bridge across the stream.'

'That's very thoughtful of you, Abdul,' said the headmaster as he patted him on the back. 'What made you think of Chuskit and her problems?'

'Azhang-ley, last week we read about the fundamental rights of citizens in our civics class. All children have a right to education. That includes Chuskit as well, doesn't it?'

'Yes, you are right, Abdul. Let me discuss this with the other teachers,' replied the headmaster.

The next day the headmaster shared Abdul's ideas with all the teachers and asked them what they felt. 'Impossible!' said one of them.

Fact File

- A 'right' refers to what a person is allowed to do.
- The Constitution of India provides a set of rights to all Indian citizens. These are called the Fundamental Rights.
- There are six Fundamental Rights. The Right to Education is one of them.

Meme-ley: 'grandfather' in Ladakhi language
Azhang-ley: a term used with respect for an elderly man in Ladakhi language
level: to make the ground even or flat

'How will Chuskit be able to write, play, and go to the toilet like the other children do?'

'That's exactly what we must work out,' said the headmaster. 'I hear that in the village of Mentok Yul, the Village Education Committee has helped build a special toilet for one of their children who cannot walk. We could ask them what they have done. But first we must get Chuskit to school. Then we could think of ways of helping her do things in school.'

Two weeks later, there was great excitement at the government school. All the children gathered outside in the playground. They came to school without their school bags: there weren't going to be any classes that day!

The teachers divided the children into groups. One group worked in front of Chuskit's house and another on the path along the stream. A third group with older children worked hard to help some of their teachers build a strong wooden bridge across the stream.

Chuskit's parents provided everyone with hot tea and biscuits. Chuskit's grandfather sat under a willow tree by the stream watching the busy schoolchildren.

'I never dreamt I'd see a day like this!' he thought to himself as he wiped a tear.

At the end of the day, it was a tired but happy group of children that returned to their homes. The path from Chuskit's home to the school was now ready!

Chuskit was going to school for the first time in her life. And that's why she was so excited!

SUMMARY

Chuskit was a little girl from Ladakh who could not walk. This made it impossible for her to go to school. Her wheelchair would get stuck on the uneven path. However, her biggest dream was to go to school. Abdul, a boy in Class 6, understood her wish. He persuaded the school headmaster to level the road and build a bridge across the stream. One day, all the students and teachers got together and worked on the road and bridge. The path was ready, and Chuskit was finally able to fulfill her dream!

COMPREHENSION

A. Mark the sentences as true (T) or false (F).

1. Chuskit got up early that morning because it was the Losar festival. ☐
2. The school was very far from Chuskit's home. ☐
3. Chuskit went to school every day by bus. ☐
4. Abdul was a student of Class 6 at the government school. ☐
5. Abdul offered to help Chuskit go to school. ☐
6. Meme-ley was unhappy that Chuskit would be able to go to school. ☐

B. Choose the correct option.

1. Chuskit had never been to school because
   a. her parents could not afford the fees.
   b. her parents felt that girls should not study.
   c. she could not walk.
2. Abdul was inspired to help Chuskit go to school because he was
   a. a sensitive boy who had read that all children have a right to education.
   b. Chuskit's friend.
   c. also differently-abled.
3. Even when she got a wheelchair, Chuskit could not go to school at first as
   a. the path to the school was too uneven and pebbly and her wheelchair could get stuck.
   b. she could not move her wheelchair for such a long distance.
   c. her parents did not allow her to go alone.

C. Read the sentences from the story and answer the questions.

1. *You can stitch better than any of them. And you draw very well.*
   a. Who says this and to whom?
   b. Why does the speaker say this?
2. *And I will be able to go wherever I want!*
   a. Who is the speaker here?
   b. Why is she/he not able to go wherever she/he wants?
   c. Why will she/he be able to go anywhere now?
3. *'I never dreamt I'd see a day like this!' he thought to himself as he wiped a tear.*
   a. Who is *he*?
   b. What is *he* thinking about?
   c. What does this show about his character?

D. Answer the questions.

1. How was Chuskit different from her cousins?
2. What did Chuskit often dream of?
3. How did Abdul help Chuskit? What does this tell us about him?
4. What had the Village Education Committee of Mentok Yul done for one of the children who could not walk?
5. Do you think Chuskit's grandfather was extremely attached to her? Support your answer with evidence from the story.
6. What do you think would have happened when Chuskit went to school for the first time? How would she have felt when she got back home?

Life Skills and Values — **Education and empathy**

1. Chuskit is finally able to go to school. How will life change for Chuskit now? Discuss.
2. Chuskit was unable to walk. What other qualities did she display that you find admirable? Share with the class.

VOCABULARY

Compound adjectives

- Read the following phrases.

  a *well-known festival* a *nine-year-old girl*

  school-going children a *kind-hearted boy*

  The words in blue are compound adjectives.
- **Compound adjectives** are made up of two or more words; they convey a single idea and add to the meaning of the nouns they modify.
- Sometimes, when a compound adjective comes before a noun, the words forming it are connected with a hyphen.

A. Fill in the blanks with the correct compound adjectives from the box.

ice-cold multi-talented snow-capped steep-sided thought-provoking well-mannered

1. .... water flowed in the stream.
2. The .... road was full of pebbles.

3. Ladakh is surrounded by .... mountains.
4. Chuskit was a .... and .... girl.
5. Abdul gave a .... idea to the headmaster.

B. Match words in Column A with words in Column B to make compound adjectives in Column C.

Column A	Column B	Column C
1. air	a. eyed	i. an .... jar
2. blue	b. fed	ii. a .... bird
3. chocolate	c. looking	iii. a .... cupcake
4. good	d. flavoured	iv. a .... actor
5. slow	e. tight	v. .... traffic
6. soft	f. powered	vi. a .... man
7. solar	g. spoken	vii. .... batteries
8. well	h. moving	viii. a .... dog

DICTIONARY SKILLS

Words in a dictionary are arranged in alphabetical order. Arrange these sets of words in alphabetical order.

1. dreamt, day, wiped, tear, wisdom
2. today, long, time, first, prayer
3. special, tea, sleep, school, tree
4. elder, everyone, carry, home, eyes

GRAMMAR

Abstract nouns

- A noun is the name of a person, animal, place, thing, or idea. Nouns can be abstract or concrete.
- A **concrete noun** is the name of something that can be felt with our sense organs. Concrete nouns can often appear in singular and plural forms. For example:

  My mother gave me two flowers.

  Children made a strong wooden bridge across the stream.
- An **abstract noun** is the name of an idea, an emotion, a quality, a state or an action. Abstract nouns cannot be felt with our sense organs. For example:

  Ama-ley had tears of happiness in her eyes.

All children have a right to education.
There was great excitement at the government school.

- Some more examples of abstract nouns are given below.

  Ideas: justice, truth, wisdom
  Emotions: happiness, love, sorrow
  Qualities: beauty, courage, kindness
  States: childhood, sickness, youth
  Actions: laughter, movement, theft

Forming abstract nouns

- Abstract nouns can be formed from other words.
  - From common nouns

    friend → friendship *mother → motherhood*
  - From verbs

    appear → appearance *break → breakage*
    clean → cleanliness *discover → discovery*
    grow → growth *realise → realisation*
  - From adjectives

    cruel → cruelty *free → freedom* *happy → happiness*
    long → length *poor → poverty* *wise → wisdom*

A. Tick the words that are abstract nouns.

1. bridge ☐
2. loyalty ☐
3. hope ☐
4. victory ☐
5. water ☐
6. wheelchair ☐

B. Change the following words into abstract nouns.

1. believe ....
2. child ....
3. honest ....
4. treat ....
5. think ....
6. true ....

Subject-verb agreement

- The verb in a sentence must agree with its subject in number.
- If the subject is singular, the verb must also be singular; if the subject is plural, the verb must also be plural. This is known as **subject-verb agreement**. For example:

  The road is too rough and uneven.
  The roads are too rough and uneven.

  In the first sentence, the subject, *the road,* is singular. Therefore, the verb used is also singular – *is*.

In the second sentence, the subject, *the roads,* is plural. Therefore, the verb used is also plural – *are.*

- We must identify whether the subject of a sentence is singular or plural so that we can use the correct form of the verb.
- When two singular subjects are joined by the conjunction *and*, they form a plural subject; so a plural verb is needed. For example:

  Chuskit and Stobdan now go to school together.

- When a phrase such as *neither..., either...,* or *one of the...* forms the subject, the subject is singular; so a singular verb is used. For example:

  One of the teachers helps Chuskit with maths work.

- When a singular subject is followed by a plural phrase, it takes a singular verb. For example:

  Abdul along with his friends is clearing the path along the stream.

- When a plural subject is followed by a singular phrase, it takes a plural verb. For example:

  The pebbles on the path were slippery.

- When two singular subjects are joined by the conjunction *or/either...or/neither...nor*, they form a singular subject; so a singular subject is needed. For example:

  Either Aba-ley or Ama-ley is providing snacks to the children.

- Some nouns look plural but are actually singular. These include names of subjects, words such as *news* and *measles,* titles of books and movies that end in *-s*. For example:

  Physics is my favourite subject.

  The news of landslides is alarming.

  Bedtime Stories is my favourite book.

- A collective noun is considered as one unit, so it takes a singular verb. For example:

  Our team has won the match.

  A herd of cows is crossing the road.

- When the emphasis is on the individual members of a group, the collective noun takes a plural verb. For example:

  The staff make a monthly contribution.

  (This sentence would sound better as: *The staff members make a monthly contribution.*)

C. Choose the correct option to fill in the blanks.

1. The little boy .... (*is/are*) unable to walk.
2. Now Chuskit, along with her brother and cousins, ... (*go/goes*) to school.
3. One of the students at the government school .... (*come/comes*) to Chuskit's home.
4. The headmaster, the teachers and the students .... (*are/is*) preparing a path from school to Chuskit's home.
5. Either my brother or my sister .... (*are/is*) coming over for my birthday.

D. Fill in the blanks with the correct form of the verb given in brackets.

1. The Constitution .... (*give*) us six Fundamental Rights.
2. All the children of this village .... (*go/goes*) to school.
3. The members of the committee for inclusive education .... (*meet*) every month.
4. The people of Ladakh .... (*celebrate*) Losar, the New Year festival, for fifteen days.
5. The decision to make a road .... (*be*) taken by the headmaster and the teachers.

LISTENING AND SPEAKING

Listening

A. Listen to the passage and mark the sentences as true (T) or false (F).

1. Eklavya was one of the Pandava princes.
2. Dronacharya taught him archery.
3. Eklavya became such an expert archer that he could hunt an animal just by hearing its sound.
4. He gave his right thumb as *guru dakshina* to Dronacharya.
5. Eklavya will always be remembered because he was a loyal disciple.

Speaking

B. Form a group of four members and role-play one of the following situations.

You are playing in a park with your friends. A visually-impaired boy comes to the park. He looks around, as if wanting to play. What would you do in this situation?

OR

An elderly lady lives in the flat next to yours. Your family often sees her struggling with her grocery and vegetable bags. Can you do something to help her?

Pronunciation

t **pronounced as** ***ch***

- Read these words in which the letter **t** is pronounced as **ch**.
  fortune (for-chune) *culture (cul-chure)*
- In most cases, when **t** is followed by *u*, it is pronounced as **ch**.
- Remember that there are some exceptions too: *tube, turn*

C. Circle the words where *t* is pronounced as *ch*.

1. constitute, mature, rapture, status, turn
2. capture, mixture, punctuation, study, Turkey
3. apparatus, fracture, picture, situation, temperature
4. tutor, nature, stupid, texture, tube
5. altitude, autumn, moisture, return, adventure

10 REDUCED INEQUALITIES

WRITING

Writing an email

The entrance of your school does not have a ramp for children with special needs. Write an email to the principal of your school, requesting her/him that such a ramp may be constructed.

Remember:

- We must be sensitive towards the needs of differently-abled people.
- The government is making efforts to create facilities for people who may need special assistance to do certain tasks.
- These include construction of ramps, lifts, etc. at public places.

File Edit View Favorites Tools Help

New Message Reply Reply All Forward Delete

To: *(email ID of the person to whom you are writing)*
Subject: *(The reason for writing)*
CC: *(Copy - if you want to send a copy of the email to someone else)*
BCC: *(Blind copy - If you want to send a copy of the email to someone without the other recipients knowing about it)*

Dear Ma'am/Sir,

Introduction: *(Clearly state the situation that exists in your school and the problems arising from it.)*

Body: *(What action you would like to request your school to take?)*

End: *(Express your gratitude in advance.)*

(The email will be written in formal language.)

Yours sincerely,

(Your full name and Class)

Done

2 In Father's Presence

Humour

OBJECTIVES

In this chapter, we will:

- *read about a young boy who cannot solve a maths problem.*
- *learn about homophones, homonyms, and homographs.*
- *learn about abbreviations.*
- *learn about the use of the present and the past continuous tenses, and modals (have to, can/can't, may).*
- *listen and complete sentences, and do a role-play.*
- *write a paragraph.*

WARM-UP

Mindfulness Activity
Maths flower puzzle

Work out a puzzle with your partner.

- Take a sheet of paper.
- Draw a large circle in the centre. Draw 5–10 petals around it to make a big flower.
- Write a 2-digit number in the centre. For example, 18.
- Write more numbers in the petals. Each number in the petals should be related to the central number. For example, you can write 36 in one petal: 18 × 2 = 36. You can write 8 in another petal. 18 −10 = 8 and so on.
- Create a flower maths puzzle for your friend. Let him/her solve it. You work out the puzzle created by your friend!
- Pin your flower puzzles on the class noticeboard.

READING

Swaminathan is unhappy. His father's courts are closed and he is certain that it could create problems with the fun he had planned to have with Rajam, Mani, Sankar and the Pea during his summer vacations. Swaminathan is proved right.

One sunny afternoon, his father, feeling that Swaminathan spends too much time playing, commands his son to stay at home, dust his books clean and sit down to study with him. Swaminathan is devastated. Read this excerpt from R. K. Narayan's Swami and Friends *and find out what follows.*

Looking Back

- An *anna* was the former currency used in India, Pakistan, and Burma. It was 1/16 of a rupee. It used to be a copper coin.
- This is how a 2 Annas coin looked!

- During British rule, the rupee was subdivided into 16 *annas*. This continued till 1957. From April 1957, each rupee had 100 *Naya Paisa*.

Swaminathan sat in his father's room in a chair, with a slate in his hand and pencil ready. Father held the arithmetic book open and dictated: 'Rama has ten mangoes with which he wants to earn fifteen annas. Krishna wants only four mangoes. How much will Krishna have to pay?'

Swaminathan gazed and gazed at this sum, and every time he read it, it seemed to acquire a new meaning. He had the feeling of having stepped into a fearful **maze**. His mouth began to water at the thought of mangoes. He wondered what made Rama fix fifteen annas for ten mangoes. What kind of a man was Rama? Probably he was like Sankar. Somehow one couldn't help feeling that he must have been like Sankar, with his ten mangoes and his **iron determination** to get fifteen annas. If Rama was like Sankar, Krishna must have been like the Pea. Here Swaminathan felt an **unaccountable** sympathy for Krishna.

'Have you done the sum?' father asked, looking over the newspaper he was reading. 'Father, will you tell me if the mangoes were ripe?'

Father regarded him for a while and **smothering** a smile remarked: 'Do the sum first. I will tell you whether the fruits were ripe or not, afterwards.'

Swaminathan felt utterly helpless. If only father would tell him whether Rama was trying to sell ripe fruits or unripe ones! Of what **avail** would it be to tell him afterwards? He felt strongly that the answer to this question contained the key to the whole problem. It would be **scandalous** to expect fifteen annas for ten

maze: a system of passages designed in a way that it is difficult to find your way through it
iron determination: great strength and desire to do something
unaccountable: strange, without any reason
smothering: (here) hiding
avail: help
scandalous: (here) shocking

unripe mangoes. But even if he did; it wouldn't be unlike Rama, whom Swaminathan was steadily beginning to hate and invest with the darkest qualities.

'Father, I cannot do the sum,' Swaminathan said, pushing away the slate.

'What is the matter with you? You can't solve a simple problem in Simple Proportion?'

'We are not taught this kind of thing in our school.'

'Get the slate here. I will make you give the answer now.'

Swaminathan waited with interest for the miracle to happen. Father studied the sum for a second and asked: 'What is the price of ten mangoes?'

Swaminathan looked over the sum to find out which part of the sum contained an answer to this question. 'I don't know.'

'You seem to be an extraordinary idiot. Now read the sum. Come on. How much does Rama expect for ten mangoes?'

'Fifteen annas of course,' Swaminathan thought, but how could that be its price, just price? It was very well for Rama to expect it in his avarice. But was it the right price? And then there was the obscure point whether the mangoes were ripe or not. If they were ripe, fifteen annas might not be an improbable price. If only he could get more light on this point!

'How much does Rama want for his mangoes?'

'Fifteen annas,' replied Swaminathan without conviction.

'Very good. How many mangoes does Krishna want?'

'Four.'

'What is the price of four?'

just price: fair or correct price
avarice: greed
obscure: something difficult to see or to understand

Father seemed to delight in torturing him. How could he know? How could he know what that fool Krishna would pay?

'Look here, boy. I have half a mind to thrash you. What have you in your head? Ten mangoes cost fifteen annas. What is the price of one? Come on. If you don't say it—'

His hand took Swaminathan's ear and gently twisted it. Swaminathan could not open his mouth because he could not decide whether the solution lay in the realm of addition, subtraction, multiplication, or division. The longer he hesitated, the more violent the twist was becoming. In the end when father was waiting with a scowl for an answer, he received only a squeal from his son.

'I am not going to leave you till you tell me how much a single mango costs at fifteen annas for ten.'

What was the matter with father? Swaminathan kept blinking. Where was the urgency to know its price? Anyway, if father wanted so badly to know, instead of harassing him, let him go to the market and find it out. The whole brood of Ramas and Krishnas, with their endless transactions with odd quantities of mangoes and fractions of money, were getting disgusting.

Father admitted defeat by declaring: 'One mango costs fifteen over ten annas. Simplify it.'

Here he was being led to the most hideous regions of arithmetic, Fractions.

'Give me the slate, father. I will find it out.' He worked and found at the end of fifteen minutes: 'The price of one mango is three over two annas.'

He expected to be contradicted any moment. But father said: 'Very good, simplify it further.'

realm: any area of activity, interest, or thought; (here) activities related to maths
harassing: (someone) troubling you for a long time
hideous: extremely ugly or unpleasant
contradicted: saying what someone has just said is wrong

It was plain sailing after that. Swaminathan announced at the end of half an hour's agony: 'Krishna must pay six annas,' and burst into tears.

At five o'clock when he was ready to start for the club, Swaminathan's father felt sorry for having worried his son all the afternoon.

'Would you like to come with me to the club, boy?' he asked when he saw Swaminathan sulking behind a pillar with a woebegone face. Swaminathan answered by disappearing for a minute and reappearing dressed in his coat and cap.

Maths Magic

You go to the market to buy 3 kg sugar. The price of sugar is ₹100 for 5 kg. How much money would you pay to buy 3 kg sugar? To do this, calculate the cost of 1 kg and multiply that by 3.

5 kg = ₹100

1 kg = $\frac{100}{5}$ = ₹20

3 kg = 20 × 3 = ₹60

So, the unitary method is a method of solving a problem by finding out the cost of 1 unit and then calculating the necessary value by multiplying the single unit. The unitary method is used to solve problems of speed, distance, time, and cost of things.

SUMMARY

Swaminathan was planning to enjoy his summer vacations with his friends. But his enjoyment did not last long. His father's courts were also closed, and he decided to brush up his son's maths. He gave Swaminathan a simple sum to solve. But the sum was about mangoes and Swaminathan got caught up in thinking about the ripeness and sweetness of the mangoes. He finally gave up. Swaminathan's father explained the method to him and even twisted his ear. Swaminathan was understandably upset. Soon, however, with his father guiding him, Swaminathan was able to solve the maths problem. Feeling sorry for his son, Swaminathan's father took him to the club for an outing.

plain sailing: extremely easy
agony: great physical or mental pain
sulking: showing your unhappiness by being silent and moody
woebegone: very sad

COMPREHENSION

A. Mark the sentences as true (T) or false (F).

1. Swaminathan's father decided to brush up his son's maths as he felt that Swaminathan was spending too much time playing. ☐
2. He gave Swaminathan a sum in which he had to calculate the cost of twenty oranges. ☐
3. Swaminathan could not solve the maths problem because he had not been taught how to do such sums in school. ☐

4. Swaminathan was keener to find out about the ripeness of the fruit rather than the cost of the fruit.
5. Father gave Swaminathan more sums to solve when he went to the club.

B. Choose the correct option.

1. Swaminathan's father decided to teach maths to his son
   a. because his courts were closed, and he had free time.
   b. just before going to the court.
   c. just after Swaminathan came back from school.
2. When Swaminathan read the problem, he began thinking
   a. about what kind of man Rama was, rather than about the problem.
   b. that the key to the solution was in the fact whether the mangoes were ripe.
   c. Both a. and b.

C. Read the sentences from the story and answer the questions.

1. *Here Swaminathan felt an unaccountable sympathy for Krishna.*
   a. Who was Krishna?
   b. Why did Swaminathan feel sympathy for him?
2. *How could that be its price, just price?*
   a. What is the price in the maths problem?
   b. Why did Swaminathan think it couldn't be a 'just price'?
3. *Here he was being led to the most hideous regions of arithmetic.*
   a. What, according to Swaminathan, was the most hideous part of maths?
   b. How was he led into that region?

D. Answer the questions.

1. Why did Swaminathan feel that the sum was like a 'fearful maze'?
2. Why did Swaminathan's father smile? Why did he have to hide his smile?
3. How did Swaminathan finally get the answer?
4. How did Swaminathan's father try to make up for his unpleasant behaviour with his son?

Life Skills and Values | **Education and reflection**

1. Swaminathan found maths difficult. What are your feelings about this subject? What makes you like or dislike a subject? Discuss.
2. Swaminathan's father is sometimes amused and sometimes strict with his son. How do you think Swaminathan was feeling in both situations? What helps you understand something better when you are taking help from a teacher/parent? Share your thoughts.

VOCABULARY

Homonyms, homophones, and homographs are words that are often confused.

Homophones

- **Homophones** are words that sound the same but have different meanings and different spellings. For example:

  to, too, two

Homonyms

- **Homonyms** are words that have the same pronunciation and spelling, but have different meanings. For example:

  bear (animal) and *bear* (to tolerate)

Homographs

- **Homographs** are words that are spelled the same but have different meanings and different pronunciations. For example:

  bow (a weapon) and *bow* (to bend)

	Same spelling	Same pronunciation	Same meaning
Homophones	×	✓	×
Homonyms	✓	✓	×
Homographs	✓	×	×

A. Choose the correct homophones to fill in the blanks.

1. He stretched .... his hands in prayer. (*forth, fourth*)
2. Shoaib stood .... and could not get a medal. (*forth, fourth*)
3. The players .... the rules of the game very well. (*new, knew*)
4. It's always nice to learn a .... sport. (*new, knew*)
5. The team wears a .... uniform. (*blue, blew*)
6. The wind .... hard, making it difficult for the player to bowl. (*blue, blew*)

B. Write sentences with the homonyms to bring out their different meanings.

1. a. fair (an event)

   ....

   b. fair (quite good)

   ....

2. a. lie (to rest in a flat position)

   ....

b. lie (to say something you know is not true)

....

3. a. kind (helpful)

....

b. kind (a type)

....

C. Each sentence has a homograph in bold. Underline the words in brackets that rhyme with the homographs.

1. The rope was **wound** around the flagstaff. *(pound/doomed)*
2. The player could not play as he received a **wound**. *(pound/doomed)*
3. The **sow** was housed comfortably in the pen. *(low/now)*
4. The farmer realised it was time to **sow** the harvest. *(low/now)*
5. The archer carefully placed the arrow on his **bow**. *(low/now)*
6. The player made a **bow** to the audience. *(low/now)*

DICTIONARY SKILLS

Abbreviations

- An abbreviation is a shortened or contracted form of a word or group of words. For example:

  Dr (doctor) Dept (department)

  e.g. (exempli gratia which means *for example)*

  etc. (et cetera which means *and other things)*

- There are two special types of abbreviations—**initialisms** and **acronyms**.

Initialism

- **Initialism** is an abbreviation formed by the first letters of a multi-word name or term. For example:

  BCCI (Board for Control of Cricket in India)

  CNG (Compressed Natural Gas)

Acronym

- An **acronym** is an abbreviation formed by the first letters of a multi-word term, and these letters are pronounced as one word. For example:

  PIN (Postal Index Number)

  UNICEF (United Nations International Children's Emergency Fund)

A. Write the abbreviations of the following.

1. Mister ....
2. Versus ....
3. World Health Organisation ....
4. Department ....

B. Write the full forms of the following abbreviations.

1. St. ....
2. BP ....
3. E.g. ....

GRAMMAR

Present continuous tense

- Continuous tenses tell us that an action continues.
- The **present continuous tense** shows that an action is happening at the moment of speaking or it is in progress. For example:

  I am preparing dinner.

  The children are playing in the garden.

Formation of the present continuous tense

<table>
<tr><td rowspan="2">Singular subject</td><td>I</td><td>am</td><td rowspan="3">+</td><td rowspan="3">-ing (present participle) form of the verb. For example: playing, dancing, reading</td></tr>
<tr><td>He/She/It</td><td>is</td></tr>
<tr><td>Plural subject</td><td>We/You/They</td><td>are</td></tr>
</table>

Past continuous tense

- The **past continuous tense** shows that an action continued for some time in the past. For example:

  I was preparing dinner.

  The puppies were sleeping at that time.

Formation of the past continuous tense

<table>
<tr><td>Singular subject</td><td>I/He/She/It</td><td>was</td><td rowspan="2">+</td><td rowspan="2">-ing (present participle) form of the verb. For example: playing, dancing, reading</td></tr>
<tr><td>Plural subject</td><td>We/You/They</td><td>were</td></tr>
</table>

A. **Look at the picture. Form sentences in both present and past continuous tenses to describe the picture.**

Present continuous:

1. ....

2. ....

3. ....

Past continuous:

1. ....

2. ....

3. ....

Modals: *have to, can/can't, may*

- Some verbs are used with another verb to ask for/give permission, show ability to do something, or show that it is necessary to do something. They are called **modals**. *Have to*, *can/can't*, and *may* are examples of modals.
- *Have to* is used to say that it is necessary to do something.

  We have to practise daily.
- *Can/can't* is used to talk about abilities.

  He can play football but he can't play tennis.
- *May* is used to ask for/give permission.

  'May I start the game?' he asked.
  You may enter the classroom.

B. Complete the sentences with *have to, can/can't, or may.*

1. Sakshi is hardworking. She .... win the first prize.
2. It is not possible. Soumesh .... participate in my place.
3. .... I borrow this book, please?
4. The participants of the Maths Olympiad .... undergo rigorous training.
5. We .... follow the rules of the debate competition.
6. Rajnish .... take part in the annual concert as he has fever.

LISTENING AND SPEAKING

Listening

A. Listen to a passage about Vedic Maths and fill in the blanks.

1. Mathematics began in India around ....
2. ...., ... and .... are some famous Indian maths scholars.
3. Indian mathematicians discovered .... and the .... system.
4. .... is the language in which ancient Indian mathematical works are written.
5. Ancient Indian mathematical works were written in the form of ....
6. The people of the Indus Valley Civilisation had a standard system of .... and invented a ....
7. People of Vedic times used large numbers and counted up to a ....

Speaking

B. Imagine your friend doesn't like maths and has not fared well in the maths test. Work in pairs and role-play to advise your friend. Reverse roles and let your friend counsel you. You may use the following phrases.

- I know how you feel…
- Maths may not appear very interesting at times…
- Maths is so useful…
- Try harder next time…
- My elder sister is so good at maths…
- My father has bought me a maths puzzle book…

WRITING

Writing a paragraph

Your summer vacations are about to begin. You have planned a lot of activities with your friends in the neighbourhood. Your parents have different ideas. They have enrolled you for a science and maths coaching class and painting lessons. What can you do in this situation to move towards a happier solution? Write down your thoughts in a paragraph.

Poem

3 Have You Earned Your Tomorrow

Universal Kindness

OBJECTIVES

In this chapter, we will:

- *read a motivating poem about helping others.*
- *learn about interrogation, a poetic device.*
- *take initiatives to help our community.*

WARM-UP

Mindfulness Activity
Breathe, recollect and narrate

Sit down, preferably cross-legged in a circle. Follow these steps.

- Close your eyes. Breathe slowly.
- Try to remember a situation when you helped someone or when someone helped you. It could be a friend, brother, sister, or your parents.
- How did you feel at that time?
- Open your eyes. If you want to talk about the incident, tell your friends and teacher about it.
- Now, how do you feel after narrating the incident?

READING

We are happy when we meet some people and don't feel quite good when we meet others. Let's read this poem by Edgar Albert Guest to find out why this happens. Can we bring joy in someone's life?

Is anybody happier because you **passed his way**?
Does anyone remember that you spoke to him today?
This day is almost over, and its **toiling time**[1] is through;
Is there anyone to utter now a kindly word of you?

Did you give a cheerful greeting to the friend who came along?
Or a **churlish** sort of 'Howdy' and then **vanish** in the **throng**?
Were you selfish pure and simple as you rushed along the way,
Or is someone mighty grateful for a deed you did today?

Can you say tonight, in **parting with the day** that's **slipping** fast,
That you helped a single brother of the many that you passed?
Is a single heart **rejoicing** over what you did or said;
Does a man whose **hopes were fading** now with courage look ahead?

Did you waste the day, or lose it, was it well or **sorely** spent[2]?
Did you leave a **trail** of kindness or a **scar** of **discontent**[3]?
As you close your eyes in **slumber** do you think that God would say,
You have **earned** one more tomorrow by the work you did today?

Literary Device

1. and 2. These are examples of **alliteration**, a literary device. The sound of the consonants, *t* in *toiling time* and *s* in *sorely spent* are repeated.
3. *scar of discontent* – This is a **metaphor**. Unhappiness has been compared to a scar and the comparison word 'like' has not been used.

passed his way: met someone
toiling time: time for working hard
churlish: unfriendly, bad-tempered, or rude
vanish: disappear
throng: a crowd of people
parting with the day: the end of day or evening time
slipping: (here) coming to an end
rejoicing: feeling happy about something
hopes were fading: losing hope
sorely: in pain
trail: way or path
scar: a mark left on your skin after a wound has healed
discontent: not being happy or satisfied
slumber: deep sleep
earned: received something because you deserve it; for example, praise

SUMMARY

In this short and simple poem, the poet gives an important message through a series of questions: Were you kind and polite to everyone you met today? Did you make someone happy? Did you help someone be brave? Even if you helped one person today, you deserve a happy tomorrow. Whether you are young or old, you can always help people through big or small deeds.

COMPREHENSION

A. Replace the underlined words with the words from the poem that are opposite in meaning to make meaningful sentences.

1. Is anyone sadder because you met him today?
2. The day has ended and sleeping time is over.
3. Did you give a churlish greeting to a friend you met?
4. Were you totally unselfish as you went about your work?
5. Is someone really ungrateful for something you did today?
6. Does a man whose hopes were rising is now feeling brave?

B. Read the lines from the poem and answer the questions.

1. *This day is almost over, and its toiling time is through*

   What does 'toiling time' refer to?

   a. a time to work

   b. a time to sleep

   c. a time to talk

2. *Can you say tonight, in parting with the day that's slipping fast,*
   That you helped a single brother of the many that you passed?

   What is slipping fast?

   a. a friend

   b. a pet dog

   c. the day

3. *Did you leave a trail of kindness or a scar of discontent?*

   What do 'trail of kindness' and 'a scar of discontent' refer to?

   a. Did you walk on a long road filled with happiness?

   b. Did you help people or did you spread unhappiness?

   c. Did many kind and happy people help you?

C. Answer the questions.

1. Write the meaning of the first stanza in two or three sentences.
2. What are the two methods of greeting people mentioned by the poet? Which one should we adopt?
3. What, according to the poet, should be our last thought before we go to sleep?

Life Skills and Values — **Interdependence and care**

1. Can we live without the help of others?
   How do our parents, teachers and friends help us?
   Share your thoughts.
2. Our every day is packed full with things we must do during the day. What are the little things that you can add to your day, where you show consideration/ sensitivity to the people around you? Discuss.

VOCABULARY

Interrogation

Interrogation or asking questions is a kind of poetic device. The poet uses it not to ask a question but to emphasise a point.

The writer knows the answer and makes sure that the reader also understands the answer from a poetic perspective.

Read this line from a famous poem.

If winter comes, can spring be far behind?

Here the poet, Shelley, knows that after winter, spring season arrives. Or after a time of sorrow comes a time of happiness. He uses interrogation only to emphasise the point for the reader.

Given below are some questions from the poem. Write the point that the poet wants to draw our attention to through these questions.

1. Did you give a cheerful greeting to the friend who came along?

   Or a churlish sort of 'Howdy' and then vanish in the throng?

2. Can you say tonight, in parting with the day that's slipping fast,

   That you helped a single brother of the many that you passed?

3. Did you waste the day, or lose it, was it well or sorely spent?

Did you leave a trail of kindness or a scar of discontent?

ACTIVITY

Group initiatives for community

Divide the class into four groups. Each group will be assigned an initiative from the list given below. Complete the projects sincerely and share your experiences with the class.

- Find out the address of a senior citizens' home in your city. Write letters or emails to the people living there.
- Talk to the non-teaching staff of your school. Have classes (once a week or so) to teach them simple conversations in English.
- Take the permission of your principal. Collect old clothes and create a 'Wall of Kindness' near your school.
- Make festival cards for Diwali, Christmas, Eid or for other special days. Send them through post to a children's home in the neighbourhood.

PROJECT 1

Traditional Martial Arts of INDIA

Have you heard of martial arts? The word *martial* means *related to fighting or war*. A martial art is a technique of fighting and self-defence.

Martial arts have also been played as sports since ancient times. Today, several martial arts are played as competitive sports. Some of them use weapons like swords and sticks, while others are played without any weapons. Judo, karate, and fencing are some examples of martial arts.

India is home to several traditional martial arts. These arts were beginning to die out as they were not practised for a long time. However, they are being revived. They have contributed to the development of some modern Asian martial arts too. Some examples of Indian martial arts are *kalarippayattu, silambam, gatka, musti yuddha* and *thang la*.

Find out about any two Indian martial arts using the Internet, books or other useful resources. Choose martial arts from different parts of the country—east, west, north, and south. Collect pictures of both the martial arts. Use an online collage making software and create two posters. Add the information that you have collected about the martial arts as text on the poster.

Remember to include the following information about each martial art.

- The name of the martial art as the heading
- A brief history of the martial art including its place of origin
- A brief description of the techniques used and skills required
- Weapons used, if any
- Its popularity and relevance today
- Drawings or pictures illustrating the martial art moves

4 Trapped

Short story

Empathy with Animals

OBJECTIVES

In this chapter, we will:

- *read a story about how animals respond to attacks and kindness.*
- *learn collocations.*
- *learn to form and use degrees of comparison.*
- *learn to use **will** and **going to** to express future time.*
- *listen to information and complete a table.*
- *do a picture analysis and identify syllables.*
- *write a report based on data interpretation.*

WARM-UP

Work in pairs and discuss the two pictures.

1. What similarities and differences do you find between the two pictures?
2. Is there a difference in how you feel when you look at the two pictures? If yes, what is it?

READING

A bear finds himself in danger after he enters a village. Read this story by Sigrun Srivastava to find out what happens to him.

The bear padded down the village path, and stopped to sniff the air. The village lay sleeping in the hot, afternoon sun. The bear walked on. He was young and chubby. Blades of grass lay knotted on his soft, shining, black fur.

When he arrived at an open gate, he peeped into a courtyard. A girl sat near a cot, scrubbing a brass plate with ash and sand. The polished plate sparkled in the midday sun. The glare hit the bear's eyes. He purred. The girl looked up. The dish fell from her hands, and she shrieked, '*Bhaloo*!'

What noise was that? The young bear was puzzled—he was frightened. He drew back a step or two. But then there was a loud noise that made him really scared.

Dogs! Barking burst out from everywhere, far and near! Suddenly, the young animal could smell danger. He turned towards the road that led through the fields back into the forest. But it was too late!

The road was not safe. It was full of humans! Their hunting cries rang in the air. The bear ran as fast as he could over open drains and a garbage dump.

Science Scan

- Bears are large mammals. There are eight living species of bears. The polar bear mostly eats meat and fish while the panda eats only plants.
- Most species of bears, except grizzly and polar bears, are shy and scared of humans.
- Three species of bears are found in India: the Himalayan black bear, the brown bear and the sloth bear.

padded: (here) walked
knotted: in knots
glare: strong, bright light
Bhaloo: a Hindi word for *bear*

But the hunters pressed in on him. Through a cloud of dust, he saw them coming towards him—a gang of children with raised sticks. And close on their heels were the dogs. 'Get him! Get him! Get him!'

The bear did not understand the cries, but the wild barking of the dogs terrified him. He turned and ran blindly—into the next lane and the next, and then into another. But his efforts were in vain. Confused with terror, he lost his way.

Now he was angry. He rushed down a lane that led into a square. The animal did not know that the square led nowhere! The square was walled in on all four sides. In the middle of it was an old, dry well. The bear got to the well in a few leaps and looked around. There was no place to hide. He was trapped!

The animal now turned round to face the children and the dogs. The children began to throw stones at him, and he was hit—first on his shoulder, then on his back. The dogs dug their teeth into his hind legs. The bear shook himself free and hit them with a paw. They fell back, and he swung round.

pressed in on him: moved towards him
on their heels: close behind them
in vain: without any useful result; without success
hind legs: the back legs of an animal
mighty: large and impressive
snarled: growled
ceased: stopped

And with one mighty leap, he disappeared into the dark depths of the well.

The children bent over the rim and threw stones and sticks into the well. The bear, angry and terrified, snarled from below. This went on for some time.

Then, all of a sudden, the stones stopped falling, and the shouts ceased. The wounded and frightened bear looked up. A single human face bent down from the top. It was the face of a girl. The bear did not know that, but he heard the girl's kind and gentle voice and felt that this was a friend. There was something in her voice that comforted him. He stopped snarling.

'That's better,' the girl said. 'Poor bear! How tired you must be! Now sit down and wait. I'll get you out of this.'

She turned round and faced the children. Everybody held her in high regard and the children knew that their bear-chase would displease her.

'Why are you torturing this animal?' she asked them. 'He has done you no harm. Go away!'

'Come on, Meera *didi*. We didn't mean any harm,' she heard someone say. 'The bear frightened the girl, and we wanted to scare him—that's all. It was just a joke.'

'I don't think so,' she said. 'Chasing a young bear into a well! Luckily, the poor bear hasn't broken his neck. Now, could you help me get him out? Can you get me a ladder?'

'I can,' said a small boy, Lakshman, and ran off. In a few minutes he was back, dragging a ladder behind him. 'I've got a ladder,' he said.

'Wonderful!' said Meera. 'This will help us rescue the trapped animal. Now, help me get it into the well. Careful! We mustn't frighten the little fellow.'

Meera looked into the well and spoke soothingly to the bear. Then, slowly and carefully, she and Lakshman lowered the ladder into the well. The little bear growled in anxiety. He clawed at the ladder wildly.

'No, no,' said Meera softly. 'It'll not hurt you. It's just a ladder! Move back, make room for the ladder!'

held her in high regard: respected her deeply
torturing: hurting physically or mentally
***didi*:** a word for 'elder sister' in Hindi and several other Indian languages
rescue: to save (somebody/something) from a dangerous or harmful situation
soothingly: trying to make someone feel better

The bear stepped back and sniffed at the ladder curiously. Slowly, he tried the first step, then another and then the third. He climbed the next six steps quickly. When he had almost reached the middle of the well, he stopped and looked up at the girl with trusting eyes.

'Come up,' she said gently. 'No one is going to hurt you.' She and Lakshman moved away from the well. 'Would the bear come up safely?' Meera wondered. Anything could happen before that. The ladder could slide off. Or it could fall forward. Or one of its rungs could break. Or...

As they watched anxiously, the head of the bear emerged above the rim of the well, and then, his shoulders. Then he sniffed, climbed onto the rim, and leapt to the ground. He looked at Meera.

'Go on, run home,' she said, smiling at him.

The bear got to his legs and bowed. Yes, he did! Lakshman saw him bow. He bowed to Meera and then padded down the lane to the main road. Once he was on the road, he ran through the large green fields back into the forest.

rungs: the bars that form steps on a ladder

SUMMARY

A young bear wandered into a village. The frightened villagers chased him and tried to catch him. The bear was terrified by the noise and the barking of dogs. As he ran, he got trapped in a square walled in on four sides, with a dry well in the middle. The bear jumped into the well to save himself. But the children kept throwing sticks and stones at him. Suddenly, the stones stopped falling and a girl's gentle voice told him not to be afraid. Meera, the kind girl, arranged for a ladder. The bear was able to climb the ladder and escape.

COMPREHENSION

A. Complete the flow chart to show the order of events in the story. You may add more boxes if needed.

B. Choose the correct option.

1. The bear sensed danger when
   a. he heard the girl's scream.
   b. he heard people shouting.
   c. he heard the barking of dogs.
2. When the bear found that the road was not safe,
   a. he ran into the jungle.
   b. he ran into a nearby river.
   c. he ran down a lane that ended in a square.
3. The bear felt trapped because
   a. the square was walled in on all sides.
   b. his feet were tied with rope.
   c. he was caught in a cage.
4. When the bear was trapped, he tried to save himself
   a. by jumping into a well in the square.
   b. by biting the children and dogs.
   c. by jumping over a fence.

C. Read the sentences from the story and answer the questions.

1. *How tired you must be! Now sit down and wait. I'll get you out of this.*
   a. Who makes this statement and to whom?
   b. Why would the listener be tired?
2. *'I've got a ladder,' he said.*
   a. Who is *he*?
   b. Why has he brought a ladder?

D. Answer the questions.

1. How did the bear realise that Meera did not mean him any harm?
2. How did the bear come out of the well?
3. What kind of girl was Meera? Support your answer with evidence from the story.
4. If Meera had not arrived there, what would have probably happened to the young bear?
5. Do you think the title of the story is a suitable one? Why/Why not?

Life Skills and Values — **Showing empathy**

1. Why do you think snakes or monkeys are attacked with sticks and stones when they enter somebody's house? What would you do in such a situation? Think and discuss.
2. Animals such as bears, monkeys, and even tigers are sometimes trained to perform tricks in the circus. Do you think it is right? Share your thoughts.

VOCABULARY

Collocations

- A *collocation* is a combination of two or more words that often go together. For example: *It's my turn to make the bed*.
- The group of words *make the bed* is a collocation. It means 'to arrange the sheets and covers on the bed'. We cannot substitute the word 'make' in this collocation with its synonyms such as 'prepare' or 'create'. Collocations are very common in English, and using the correct collocation is important.
- There are different types of collocations. The collocation *make the bed* is a *verb* + *noun collocation*. Here are some more examples of verb + noun collocations.

break a promise	*break a record*
do a favour	*do the shopping*
have a bath	*have a holiday*
make a fortune	*make a mistake*
take a decision	*take a message*

In these examples, one verb may be used with many nouns to form verb + noun collocations.

A. Match the verbs and nouns to form collocations.

Column A	Column B
1. come	a. a chat
2. get	b. a difference
3. have	c. a job
4. make	d. an opportunity
5. miss	e. to an end

B. Form verb + noun collocations with the nouns given below and make sentences. One is done for you.

1. a party: Let us have a party to celebrate our success.
2. a phone call: ....
3. advice: ....
4. an email: ....
5. an exam: ....
6. an opinion: ....

Degrees of comparison

- Adjectives have three forms—positive, comparative, and superlative. These forms are also called degrees. For example:

Positive	Comparative	Superlative
big	bigger	biggest
unusual	more unusual	most unusual

- The positive form is used to describe a person or thing. For example:

  My sister is tall. *The book is interesting.*

- The comparative form is used for comparing two people or things. For example:

  My sister is taller than my mother. *The book was more interesting than the film.*

- The superlative form is used for comparing three or more persons or things within a group. For example:

  My sister is the tallest girl in her class. *This is the most interesting book I've ever read.*

Spelling rules for comparatives and superlatives

- To make the comparative form, we add the suffix *-er* to the adjective in the positive form.
- To make the superlative form, we add the suffix *-est* to the adjective in the positive form. For example:

Positive	Comparative	Superlative
big	bigger	biggest
clever	cleverer	cleverest

- Some adjectives are irregular. Their comparative and superlative forms are different words altogether. For example:

Positive	Comparative	Superlative
bad	worse	worst
good	better	best
little	less	least

- A few adjectives form their comparative forms by adding *more/less* before them and their superlative forms by adding *most/least* before them. For example:

Positive	Comparative	Superlative
difficult	more difficult	most difficult
useful	less useful	least useful

A. Complete the table with the adjectives in their three forms of comparison.

Positive	Comparative	Superlative
1.	....	fastest
2. hot	....	....
3.	....	most colourful
4.	nicer	....
5.	smarter	....
6. important	....	....
7.	....	funniest
8.	less spicy	....

B. Fill in the blanks with the correct form of the adjectives in brackets.

1. It was the .... (*big*) bear I had ever seen.
2. Lakshman brought a .... (*long*) ladder.
3. The young bear was .... (*frightened*) than ever before.
4. The weather this summer has been .... (*bad*) than last year because the forest has been cut down.
5. Martha is .... (*industrious)* than any other girl in the class.
6. Technology has made shopping .... *(easy)* and .... *(fast)*.

Will and *going to* for future time

- *Will* and *going to* are used when we refer to the future.
- *Will* + **verb** is used to:
  - make predictions or talk about things that are certain to happen.

    Our school team will win.
  - show willingness to do something or make a promise.

    I will help you write the report.
- **Am/is/are** + *going to* + verb is used to
  - talk about a plan or decision already made for the future.

    I am going to watch the film this weekend.
  - show intention.

    They are going to buy tickets for the match.
  - show that something is likely to happen.

    It is going to rain.

C. Match each situation with the correct speech bubble.

He will win the race.

Aiza will teach you how to play tennis.

Rishabh will take part in the obstacle race.

We have done it once and we will do it again.

D. Respond to these situations with *be going to*. Use the verb given in brackets. One is done for you.

1. There is no milk for the team. (*get*)
   Okay, I am going to get some.
2. The sky is overcast. (*rain*)
   ....
3. The phone is ringing. (*answer*)
   ....
4. The players want water. (*arrange for*)
   ....
5. The players land in Brazil tonight. (*meet*)
   ....
6. The cricket equipment is too heavy for me to move it alone. (*ask for help*)
   ....

LISTENING AND SPEAKING

Listening

A. Listen to a passage on tigers and fill in the missing parts in the two columns.

Column A	Column B
1. Weight of an adult tiger	....
2.	25,000 acres of forest
3. Number of tigers in the wild a hundred years ago	....
4. Number of tigers in the wild today	....
5.	Half of all tiger cubs
6.	Term for a group of tigers
7. Two reasons for tiger becoming an endangered species	....

Speaking

21st Century Skills — Critical Thinking

B. Have you ever thought about the problems faced by stray animals? In groups, articulate your thoughts on seeing the picture.

Pronunciation

Syllables

- A **syllable** is a single unit of speech into which a word is divided.
- It contains a **single vowel sound** and one or more consonants.
- A consonant sound alone cannot form a syllable but a vowel alone can form a whole syllable on its own.
- A word may have one, two, or more syllables.
- A word is separated into syllables when it is spoken. For example:

  The word **forest** has two syllables: *for* and *est*.

  These can be marked as *for/est* or *for.est*.

  The word **over** has two syllables: o/*ver*.
- In most dictionaries, syllable breaks are marked.

A. Say these words aloud.

One syllable	Two syllables	Three syllables
tree	chil.dren	af.ter.noon
well	some.one	a.ni.mal
bridge	hair.brush	fur.ni.ture
grand	Mon.day	pho.to.graph
whale	base.ment	tri.an.gle

B. Break these words into syllables. You may consult a dictionary, if needed.

1. classroom ....
2. difficult ....
3. grass ....
4. morning ....
5. shoulder ....
6. victor ....
7. playground ....
8. monster ....
9. alligator ....
10. government ....

WRITING

Data Interpretation

Look at the two bar diagrams. The first shows the number of animal species that are threatened or endangered in India (given in numbers). The second shows the major reasons for this (given in percentages). Write a short report based on the given data.

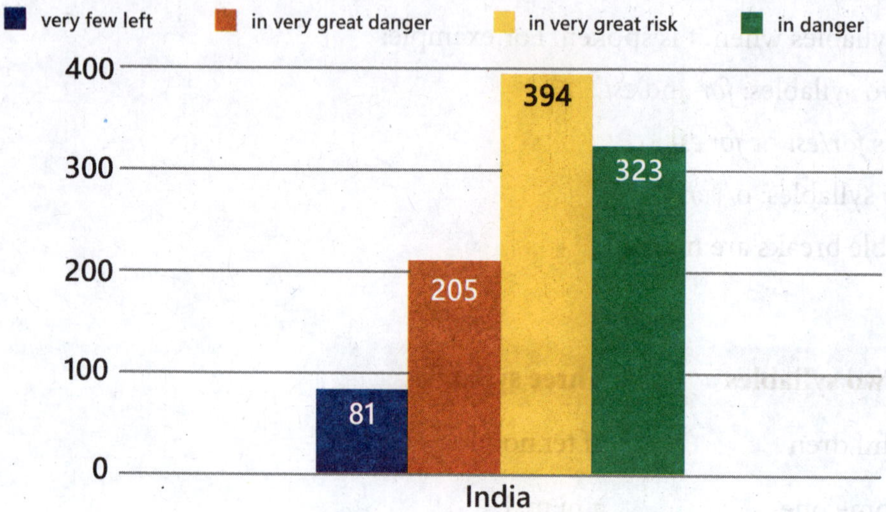

Major threats to animal populations

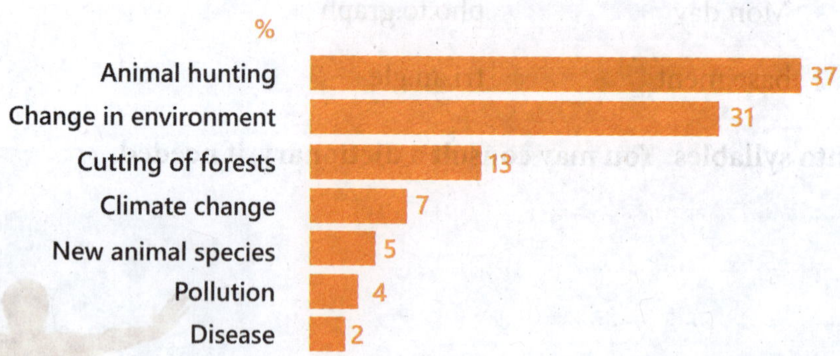

Hint:

Source: IUCN

- Organise your report in two paragraphs. The first paragraph should give the number of animal species that are in different categories of danger.

  Animal species in India are in danger. The first bar graph shows us...

- The second paragraph can talk about the reasons why animal species in India are on the verge of extinction. Remember to write the percentage with the reason.

  The second bar graph clearly shows why the animal species in India face extinction, if not stopped. The biggest reason...

5 Underground

Earth and Creatures

OBJECTIVES

In this chapter, we will:

- *read a poem that describes scientific facts in an imaginative way.*
- *learn about similes.*
- *create and play an animal quiz.*
- *distinguish between the right and wrong ways of treating animals.*

WARM-UP

Different animals have different habitats. Some animals live under the ground most of the times. Look at the pictures. Write the names of these animals.

1. ....
2. ....
3. ....
4. ....
5. ....

READING

Read this poem by James Reeves to learn about life under the ground.

In the deep kingdom underground
There is no light and little[1] sound.
Down below the earth's green floor
The rabbit and the mole explore.

The quarrying ants run to and fro
To make their populous empires grow.
Do they, as I pass overhead
Stop in their work to hear my tread?

Some creatures sleep and do not toil
Secure and warm beneath the soil.
Sometimes a fork or spade intrudes
Upon their earthly solitude.

Downwards the branching tree roots spread
Into the country of the dead.
Deep down[2] the buried rocks and stones
Are like earth's gigantic bones[3].
In the dark kingdom underground
How many marvelous things are found.

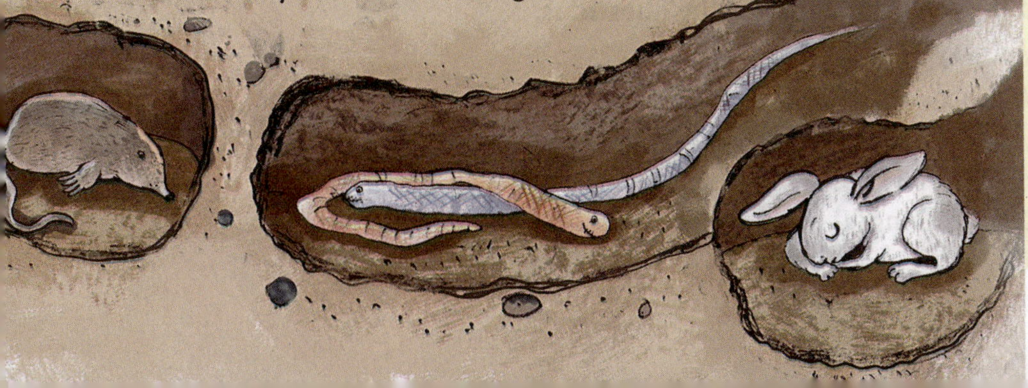

Literary Device

1. The consonant sound *l* is repeated. This is called **alliteration.**
2. The repetition of the consonant sound *d* is another example of alliteration in this poem.
3. This is a **simile**. Rocks and stones are being compared to bones.

Earth Speak

- The earth is made up of three main layers: crust, mantle, and core.
- The crust is the outermost and thinnest layer.
- The distance to the centre of the earth from its surface is 6,371 kms.

Science Scan

- Adaptation is the way of changing something to make it suitable for a particular situation.
- Animals like ants, earthworms, moles, and rabbits are adapted to live underground.
- Some insects and animals living underground live alone. Others live in groups. Ants live in large groups called colonies.

quarrying: (here, ants) digging out mud from the earth
to and fro: (going) from one place to another and back
populous: having many inhabitants
tread: the sound of footsteps
intrudes: disturbs
solitude: being alone and peaceful
gigantic (pronounced *jaigantic)*: very big; huge

SUMMARY

When one looks at the earth's surface, it is hard to imagine that down below, where no light or sound enters, there is a huge kingdom of animals. Under the ground, live rabbits, moles, and large colonies of ants. Some work hard while others sleep (hibernate). Only when a human being walks on the ground above or digs a hole are the animals disturbed. The roots of the trees also spread deep into the earth.

COMPREHENSION

A. Fill in the blanks with words from the poem.

1. Underground life has been described as a .... by the poet.
2. It is populated by many animals such as ...., ..., and ....
3. The .... of the trees spread into the .... of the dead.
4. Many .... things are found under the ground.

B. Choose the correct option.

1. The poet says
   a. there are many creatures under the ground.
   b. there are buildings under the ground.
   c. many precious stones are buried under the ground.
2. The phrase that shows that ants live together is
   a. 'to and fro'.
   b. 'quarrying ants'.
   c. 'populous empires'.
3. How do some sleeping animals get disturbed?
   a. By the ants rushing by
   b. By the rabbits and moles that live there
   c. By the humans digging with a spade or a fork
4. The underground has been called the 'country of the dead' because
   a. the dead are buried in graves in some cultures.
   b. dead leaves and animals get buried in the soil.
   c. Both a. and b.

C. Read the lines from the poem and answer the questions.

1. *Do they, as I pass overhead*
   Stop in their work to hear my tread?
   a. Who are 'they' and what work are they doing?
   b. What do they hear?
   c. What is the speaker doing?

2. *Some creatures sleep and do not toil*
   a. What could these creatures be?
   b. Why do they 'not toil'?
   c. The poet makes a comparison of these creatures and others who 'toil'. How are their lives different?

3. *Deep down the buried rocks and stones*
   Are like earth's gigantic bones.
   a. What do the buried rocks and stones appear to be to the poet?
   b. Do you think this comparison is suitable? Explain.

D. Answer the questions.

1. Write five adjectives to describe the kind of life that exists underground.
2. The poet vividly describes many things. Which description(s) do you like the most and why?
3. Does the poem inspire you to dig underground and discover the marvellous world that exists underground? Give reasons for your answer.

Life Skills and Values — **Caring for environment**

Non-biodegradable wastes such as plastic is extremely harmful to the soil. It is also dangerous for animals and insects living above or below the ground. What must we do to help animals make their underground homes safer? Share your ideas in the class.

VOCABULARY

Similes

- A **simile** is a figure of speech which involves the comparison of one person or thing with another.
- The two people or things compared with each other are completely different.
- A simile is used to make the description more emphatic and clear.
- Similes use the word 'like' or 'as'. For example:

  *The soldier was **as brave as a lion**.*

Here, the soldier and the lion are very different but their courage or bravery is similar.

- In the following lines from the poem, the rocks under the earth are being compared to bones in a body. This is a simile.

  Deep down the buried rocks and stones

  Are like earth's gigantic bones.

A. Identify the similes in the following sentences. Say what is being compared.

1. Tony is as meek as a lamb.
2. My dog follows me like my shadow.
3. I am as blind as a bat without my spectacles.
4. My brother is as slow as a snail in doing his homework.
5. Today is the last exam. From tomorrow, I will be as free as a bird!

B. Rewrite the sentences using similes from the box. One is done for you.

as a bear *as a bull* *as ice* *~~as a sloth~~* *as lightning*

1. Varun is lazy. Varun is as lazy as a sloth.
2. Rohan was hungry. ....
3. Rajshree was very angry. ....
4. Her hands were very cold. ....
5. My Internet connection is fast. ....

C. Many commonly used similes compare people to animals. What adjective/quality is associated with these animals? One is done for you.

1. bee as busy as a bee
2. eel ....
3. mule ....
4. owl ....
5. ox ....

ACTIVITY

21st CENTURY SKILLS ICT

Creating and playing a quiz

A. Go on the Internet and create a quiz on the topic 'Know Your Animals'.

- Choose five animals.
- Write a brief description about each animal in 2-3 sentences.
- If you use online application like Quizlet, you can write the description on the flashcards.
- Choose a partner and quiz him/her.

Treating animals the right way

21st Century Skills
Critical Thinking

B. Read the statements on different ways of treating animals. Are they kind or unkind? Write their number in the correct column. In the last column, give the reason for your choice.

Remember this golden rule:

Do unto others as you would have them do unto you.

1. Animals should be kept in zoos.
2. Pet dogs should be kept unchained.
3. We should provide shelter to stray animals during harsh weather.
4. It is okay to hit a pet if it dirties our carpet.
5. We should dissect frogs and earthworms to learn zoology.
6. Animals should be allowed to stay in their natural habitats.
7. A petting zoo is a great idea to teach children to love animals.
8. Animals like snakes, bears, and monkeys can be trained to perform tricks.
9. If we see a hurt animal on the street, we should take it to a vet with our parents' help.

Kind to animals	Unkind to animals	Why?

6 Healing the Hills

Saving the Planet

OBJECTIVES

In this chapter, we will:

- *read about the degradation of the Western Ghats.*
- *learn phrasal verbs and its usage.*
- *learn adjectives ending in -ing and -ed.*
- *learn adverbs, its type and its usage.*
- *listen to information and complete a form.*
- *role-play a situation.*
- *write an article and an acrostic poem.*

WARM-UP

Mindfulness Activity
Peaceful interactions

A. Are you ready for some nature-filled activity? Go ahead and enjoy yourself.

- You are in your school garden. Sit on the grass. Close your eyes. Touch the grass. How does it feel?
- Get up and go near a plant growing in the garden. Touch it gently. Be careful not to hurt the plant. Speak or sing to the plant. Do you feel happy? Is the plant happy that you are near?
- Go to a tree. Feel its bark. Lean against it. Hug it. What/How do you feel? Do you think the tree is able to sense your touch, your love?

B. Forests are called 'the lungs of the Earth' as they purify the air. Write down four things we get from forests.

1. .... 2. ....

3. .... 4. ....

READING

12 RESPONSIBLE CONSUMPTION AND PRODUCTION

Rich in animal and plant species, the Western Ghats are hills that are being destroyed by us humans—we are cutting down trees and building cities and roads. Many efforts are being made to save the hills but are they enough?

The beautiful Western Ghats

The Western Ghats span a hilly stretch of 1,600 kilometres that runs parallel to the western coast of India.

It is a mountain range, that dates back to 150 million years, and passes through six states in India – Gujarat, Maharashtra, Goa, Karnataka, Kerala, and Tamil Nadu.

This region is covered with dense evergreen forests, deciduous forests, grasslands, and tropical rainforests. It boasts of over 9,000 varieties of plants, 139 mammal species, 508 kinds of birds, several types of amphibians, insects, reptiles, and freshwater fish.

This area also receives abundant rain and is the source of perennial rivers like the Godavari, Krishna, Kaveri, and Tungabhadra.

Dotted with enchanting hill stations, wildlife sanctuaries and traditional sacred groves, this entire region is also a UNESCO World Heritage Site.

These hills are alive!

This incredible and historic site is the Western Ghats or the *Sahyadri* Mountains.

The benevolent one

The word, *Sahyadri*, means 'benevolent' or 'generous'. These mountains are generous in what they have given us and continue to do so, despite the harm we are doing to these kind hills.

The Western Ghats block the monsoon winds from the Arabian Sea and cause heavy rainfall. The sun rays falling on these slopes help in the plentiful growth of vegetation. These two factors

Earth Speak

- Deciduous forests are forests with trees that shed their leaves either in autumn or in summer.
- The leaves grow again in spring or in rainy season.
- These trees have flat broad leaves.

parallel: two lines or objects that are the same distance apart along the whole of their length
abundant: in large quantities
perennial: lasting for many years

Fact File

- Sacred groves are ancient forests protected by tribal people living there.
- The tribes believe that Gods live in these forests.
- They protect the forests fiercely and take only what is necessary for them.

together account for the remarkable diversity of life forms found here. It is also the reason why five rivers originate here. This, in turn has formed the unique climate and the soil of this area. This region, thus, sustains millions of people in peninsular India through the water of its rivers, the food grown here, and the livelihood provided by its jungles.

These forests are responsible for one-fourth of the rainfall in peninsular India and help to keep the temperatures down. They are also carbon sinks protecting us from the disastrous effects of climate change. Several species of flora and fauna are endemic to this region. 30 per cent of all plants and animals of India are found here, including rare medicinal plants.

Unbelievable, isn't it? One would think such a treasure trove would be a strictly guarded area.

Hurting the hills

Far from protecting this wealth, we are robbing it—ourselves. And the inflicted wounds are deep. The Ghats have shrunk by 25 per cent.

The creation of cities has led to loss of habitat for plants and animals. Building of cities and harmful factories continue without any planning.

The forests are also being cleared for an ever-growing network of roads and rails.

Science Scan

- A carbon sink is any natural environment that absorbs more carbon dioxide than it releases.
- The natural carbon sinks are plants, oceans, and soil.
- The amount of carbon in the atmosphere is rising because humans use petrol, keep scores of livestock and cut down trees.
- If carbon levels rise, the temperature of the earth will also rise.

The beautiful Western Ghats

diversity: variety
disastrous: disastrous effects cause harm to people or place
endemic: belonging to a particular place
inflicted: made someone experience something unpleasant

Another problem is the construction of dams on the rivers for electricity and irrigation. The dams destroy the ecosystems that exist around the rivers. The dams have created reservoirs that have flooded many forests.

Hectares of land has been brought under cultivation by felling trees, again reducing forests. Alien species of plants, such as eucalyptus, acacia, and lantana, have been introduced here. These species are destroying the native plants, and reducing food supply for the native plant-eating animals. This affects the entire food chain here.

Eucalyptus leaves

Lantana

Acacia

Mining, often unregulated and sometimes illegal, is ruining the hills. The strong vibrations caused by explosives used in mining is shaking the very foundations of the forests.

The forests, the animals, the climate, the soil, the rivers—all are under severe threat.

Healing the Hills

According to the World Wildlife Fund (WWF) survey, the Western Ghats need immediate protection.

Many steps have been taken by the government and the people to heal the hills.

The Ministry of Environment and Forests of India has declared several areas of the Ghats as wildlife sanctuaries, biosphere reserves and national parks. The ministry also appointed the Western Ghats Ecology Expert Panel (WGEEP) in 2010 to study the problems.

The Silent Valley Movement, 1976 was started by school teachers to save the Silent Valley in Kerala. A dam was going to be made over the Kunthipuzha River and would have flooded the forest in the Silent Valley. The movement was successful and the area was declared the Silent Valley National Park in 1985.

Peaceful Society, an NGO, decided to organise a march in 1987–88 through the Western Ghats to understand the problems. 169 men and women from 11 states and 4 countries took part and marched along the length of the Ghats. The findings of the participants were put together and discussed in a conference in Goa later.

reservoirs: artificial lakes formed when dams are made
lantana: a small flowering shrub, belonging to America and Africa. Their leaves are poisonous to most animals.
unregulated: not following the law
biosphere reserves: places where plants and animals are protected by law passed by the government

The Ghats were declared an ecological hotspot in 1988 through the efforts of British biologist, Norman Myers.

Appiko is the Kannada word for 'hugging'. The Appiko Movement was started by Panduranga Hegde of Karnataka. In the 1980s, he led people to stop cutting of trees by hugging them. The slogan of the movement is *Ubsu* (save), *Belesu* (grow) and *Balasu* (rational use).

People hugging trees during the Appiko Movement

In November 2014, the government of Maharashtra decided to build a shed for the Mumbai Metro Rail in the Aarey Forest in western Mumbai. This would mean cutting down over 2000 trees. The citizens of Mumbai came together and started 'Save Aarey Movement'. After a long battle, the government reversed its decision.

Critical Ecosystems Partnership Fund (CEPF) along with Ashoka Trust for Research in Ecology and the Environment (ATREE) are doing extensive work for conserving the Ghats by creating an information bank about the hills.

reversed: changed
extensive: huge
landslides: large amounts of earth and rocks falling down the side of a mountain

Is it enough?

The 2018 floods and landslides in Kerala that resulted in the death of several people and destruction of property are directly linked to the damage done to the Western Ghats, according to ecologist Madhav Gadgil, chairman of WGEEP.

The amount of rainfall, the path taken by rivers and the climate across large areas have already changed.

Animal poaching continues.

The Western Ghats are the lifeline for peninsular India. The tremendous bio-richness of this mountain range makes it priceless. Only through restoring them can we put a stop to the terrible floods and landslides and rising temperatures.

> **poaching:** hunting animals without permission
> **restoring:** getting something back to its original state

Let's come together and promise to do our little bit in showing gratitude for the *Sahyadri*, the Benevolent One.

SUMMARY

The Western Ghats is a long mountain range along the western coast of India and is extremely rich in biodiversity with hundreds of species of flora and fauna. It receives a lot of rainfall and many rivers originate here. These hills are vital for India in several ways. Unfortunately, because of cutting of trees, building of cities, constructing of dams and factories, these hills are being destroyed and many species of plants and animals have been declared endangered. Both the government and the people have been taking various measures to protect the hills but still much more remains to be done.

COMPREHENSION

A. Fill in the blanks.

1. The Western Ghats run parallel to the .... of India.
2. These hills were born about .... years ago.
3. Another name for the Western Ghats is the ....
4. About .... per cent of the plants and animals of India are found here.
5. 'Appiko' is a Kannada word which means ....

B. Choose the correct option.

1. The Western Ghats pass through
   a. six states of India, namely Delhi, Jammu and Kashmir, Punjab, Haryana, Uttar Pradesh and Uttarakhand.
   b. four states of India, namely West Bengal, Odisha, Madhya Pradesh and Bihar.
   c. six states in India, namely Gujarat, Maharashtra, Goa, Karnataka, Kerala and Tamil Nadu.

2. There are many species of plants and animals in these hills because
   a. this area receives a lot of rainfall.
   b. this area gets plenty of sunshine.
   c. Both a. and b.
3. Peaceful Society, an NGO, organised
   a. the Silent Valley Movement in Kerala.
   b. a march through the Western Ghats to understand the problems.
   c. the Save Aarey Movement in Mumbai.

C. Read the article and answer the questions.

1. *These hills are alive!*
   a. Which hills is the writer referring to?
   b. Why are they said to be 'alive'?
2. *This affects the entire food chain.*
   a. What affects the entire food chain?
   b. How is it being affected?
3. *Another problem is the construction of dams on the rivers...*
   a. Why are dams being built on the rivers?
   b. Why does the writer say they cause problems?

D. Answer the questions.

1. The place where a river begins is called its source. Why are the Western Ghats the source of five rivers? Which rivers are these?
2. How does this region sustain millions of people?
3. Why does the writer say that we are hurting these kind hills?
4. Why was the Silent Valley Movement started? Who started it?
5. What is the slogan of the Appiko Movement? What do people of this movement do to help the hills?
6. What was the aim of the Save Aarey Movement? Was the movement successful?

Life Skills and Values — **Nature conservation**

1. Conservation of environment is not a one-man job. Do you agree? Share your thoughts.
2. Do you often go to a park or a garden? What do you do there? How do you feel when you go there? Talk about your experience.

VOCABULARY

Phrasal verbs

- A **phrasal verb** is a combination of a verb and a preposition or adverb.
- The addition of the preposition or adverb to the verb changes the meaning of the verb.
- Read the following sentence.

  Hectares of land has been brought under cultivation by felling trees.

  Bring under is a phrasal verb. It means to put something under the management of someone. Here it means that a large forest area was cleared and is used to grow crops now.

Many phrasal verbs are possible with the verb, *bring*. For example:

- *At first, he didn't believe that forests are important, but I managed to bring him around to my opinion.*
  (change someone's opinion)
- *They brought forward the date of the conference so that they could start their work.*
  (change the date or time of an event so that it happens earlier)
- *Marooty Motors will bring out a new, environmentally-friendly car this year.*
  (produce a new product)

A. Fill in the blanks with the correct phrasal verbs from the box.

break into   *call off*   *do without*   *hand over*   *slow down*   *think over*

1. Don't drive so fast. Please ....
2. What will we ever .... trees!
3. The burglars used a ladder to .... the house.
4. Before you leave, please .... all the files to me.
5. The manager asked her secretary to .... the meeting.
6. My mother needs some time to .... the picnic proposal.

B. Match the phrasal verbs with their meanings.

Phrasal verb	Meaning
1. run into	a. to remove something
2. run out	b. to continue doing something
3. carry on	c. to have no more of something
4. carry out	d. to meet someone unexpectedly
5. take after	e. to start doing an activity or a job
6. take away	f. to look or behave like a family member

GRAMMAR

Adjectives ending in *-ing* and *-ed*

- Some words ending in *-ing* and *-ed* appear to be verbs but function as adjectives. For example:

  enchanting hill stations *inflicted wounds* *unregulated mining*

  The word *enchanting* describes the noun hill station, the word *inflicted* describes wounds and the word *unregulated* describes mining. They are adjectives.
- Adjectives ending in *-ing* and *-ed* may show whether an action is continuing or is over.
- An *-ing* adjective shows that an action is continuing.

  In *enchanting* hill station, *enchanting* shows that the hill station continues to be enchanting.
- An *-ed* adjective shows that an action is over.

  In *inflicted* wounds, *inflicted* shows that the wounds have already been inflicted.

  In *unregulated* mining, *unregulated* shows that the mining is not controlled by the authorities.
- Adjectives ending in-*ing* and *-ed* may also show feelings.
- An *-ing* adjective describes a person, a thing, or a situation that causes a feeling.

  I saw a frightening documentary on the Western Ghats.

  In *frightening documentary*, the documentary causes the feeling of fright.
- An-*ed* adjective shows that the person being described has the feeling.

  The horrified tribal leader walked along the river.

  In *horrified* tribal leader, it is the leader who feels horrified.

A. Choose the correct adjective to fill in each blank.

1. The .... (*shocking/shocked*) news of the floods in Kerala made the whole country sad.
2. The environmentalist gave a very .... (*inspiring/ inspired*) speech.
3. Suman found the trek in the Western Ghats quite .... (*fascinating/fascinated*).
4. The .... (*frightening/frightened*) villagers could not go to the jungle at night.
5. The .... (*confusing/confused*) man did not know how to put out the forest fire.
6. The .... (*exciting/excited*) children enjoyed the jungle safari.

B. Add the suffix *-ed* or *-ing* to the words in the box. Then, fill in the blanks correctly with the words formed.

alarm	*interest*	*reward*	*surprise*	*terrify*	*trouble*

1. Deforestation is happening at a/an .... rate.
2. Flash floods cause .... destruction.
3. Saurabh was greatly .... when he heard about the landslide.
4. Riyaz was .... when he read the book about the Ghats.
5. The modern generation is keenly .... in the conservation of the environment.
6. The success of the Appiko Movement has been very ....

Adverbs

- **Adverbs** are words that tell us how, when, and where an action is performed.
- Adverbs add to the meaning of verbs.
- Read the following sentences. The words in italics are verbs. The words in green are adverbs.

  These species are *slowly destroying* the native plants. (how)

  These two factors together account for the remarkable diversity of life forms *found here*. (where)

  The findings of the participants were *discussed* in a conference in Goa *later*. (when)
- Adverbs also modify adjectives.

  The citizens were *very angry* when they learnt about the Metro car shed to be built in the forest. (*very* modifies *angry*)

  The news about the Kerala floods was *extremely shocking*. (*extremely* modifies *shocking*)
- Adverbs that answer the question 'how' are called adverbs of manner. For example:

  quickly, *sweetly*, *gracefully*, *happily*

  The members of the Appiko Movement *hugged* the trees *tightly*.
- Adverbs that answer the question 'where' are called adverbs of place. For example:

  here, *there*, *everywhere*, *somewhere*, *outside*

  Five perennial rivers like the Godavari, Krishna, Kaveri and Tungabhadra *start* from *there*.
- Adverbs that answer the question 'when' are called adverbs of time. For example:

  now, *never*, *first*, *early*, *yesterday*, *later*, *today*

  The participants of the Silent Valley Movement *got* success *last year*.

C. Underline the adverbs in the sentences.

1. A tree plantation drive was announced yesterday.
2. We must actively participate in this programme.
3. Let's plant some more saplings here.
4. We will meet the forest officials tomorrow.
5. We must not disturb the goats grazing nearby.
6. Trees play a very important role in protecting our environment.

D. Fill in the blanks with adverbs from the box.

fast	*first*	*loudly*	*lovingly*	*tomorrow*

1. Reema patted her favourite tree ....
2. Dr Gadgil, the ecologist, was invited to speak ....
3. Gauri, the village elder, spoke ....
4. We will go to the landfill .... to see what can be done.
5. The protesters moved ....

LISTENING AND SPEAKING

Listening

A. Listen to a passage about a well-known Indian environmentalist and complete the form.

1. Name ....
2. Date of birth ....
3. Place of birth ....
4. Place where he studied in 1945 ....
5. Name of wife ....
6. Movement started for tree protection ....
7. The dam he opposed ....
8. Awards received in

   a. 1981 .... b. 1986 .... c. 2009 ....

Speaking

B. You wish to go to Auli for skiing but your parents think that you are too young to learn skiing. Work in pairs and take turns to role-play a parent and a child. Put forth convincing arguments.

Tips for the role-play

- Be clear about the role you are playing.
- Present your facts clearly.
- Listen carefully to the other party.
- Be sure of what you want, yet be flexible.
- Be courteous and use polite language.

Some useful words and phrases:

- I understand what you say but I feel...
- I have found that...
- A friend of mine who has been there tells me...
- Just think about...

WRITING

Writing an article

A. Your school organised a tree plantation drive on 15 August. Write an article for your school magazine, in not more than 150 words, giving all the details of the event.

Read the information given below. This will make it easier for you to write the article.

what
- Tree Plantation Day

when
- 15th August
- 10 a.m.

where
- in an open ground near our school

why

the ground does not have any trees

how

the Principal, ten teachers, and twenty-five students from the Green Brigade Club got saplings from a government nursery

An acrostic poem

An acrostic poem is a fun way to write poetry. The first letter in each line will form a word which is the title or theme of the poem. All the lines are related to the topic. Read this acrostic poem on trees.

TREES

Trees are God's gift to us
Respecting this gift is our duty
Energising the environment is what trees do
Every other need of ours they fulfil too
Saviours they are for me and you.

B. Write an acrostic poem on any one of the following topics.

forest hills land rain

....
....
....
....
....
....
....
....
....
....
....
....
....
....
....
....
....

Now, create a 2-slide PowerPoint presentation with the poem, adding some relevant pictures from the web or a drawing you made.

Poem

7 Awareness About Our Environment

Environmental Conservation

OBJECTIVES

In this chapter, we will:

- *read and understand a poem on the condition of the environment.*
- *learn about imagery.*
- *study a decomposing timeline of certain items.*
- *learn about biodegradable and non-biodegradable wastes.*

WARM-UP

Form groups of three. Each group must choose a picture and write 2-3 sentences about it. Then, discuss it in class.

1.

2.

3.

- ....
- ....
- ....

READING

Read this thought-provoking poem by Sylvia Stults, who asks us whether we are aware of what we are doing to our environment.

Broken bottles[1] and charred pieces of glass
Wadded up newspapers tossed on the grass
Pouring of concrete and tearing out trees[2]
This is the environment that surrounds me?

Poisons and insecticides sprayed on our food
Oceans filling with thick oil crude
All sea life destined to a slow awful doom
These are the things we are to consume?

Mills pumping out iron expelling yellow fumes
Airlines emitting caustic gases from fuels
Weapons of destruction tested at desolate sites
And this is the air that's to sustain life?

There has to be something that someone can do
Like raise the awareness to those around you
That if we don't heed the problem at hand
It's your life that's at stake, the destruction of man.

Literary Device

1. and 2. The consonant sound *b* is repeated in *broken bottles* and the sound *t* is repeated in *tearing out trees*. Such a repetition of a sound is called **alliteration**.

Science Scan

- Crude oil is a dark liquid that is found deep inside the earth. Millions of years ago, the oceans were filled with animals and plants. When these died and fell to the bottom of the oceans, they were buried under layers of sand and mud. Under heat and pressure, their remains turned into what we call crude oil and natural gas.

charred: burnt and black
wadded up: rolled into a tight bundle
concrete: building material made by mixing together cement, sand, small stones, and water
insecticides: poisonous chemicals used to kill insects
oil crude: (crude oil) oil in its natural state, before it is refined in factories to make petrol and diesel
consume: to eat or drink
expelling: throwing out with force
fumes: smoke, gas, or something similar that smells strongly or is dangerous to breathe in
emitting: producing or giving out
caustic gases: chemical substances that are very powerful and can destroy or dissolve other substances
at stake: that can be won or lost, depending on the success of a particular action

SUMMARY

The poet is deeply disturbed about the state of the environment and asks us to be aware of what we are doing to it. When she looks around, she sees broken bottles, old newspapers, stumps of trees, and concrete structures. The food is full of poisonous chemicals and the oceans are filled with crude oil. The air is polluted by the toxic gases from factories and tests of nuclear weapons. She urges us to wake up and do our bit towards the environment.

COMPREHENSION

A. Fill in the blanks with words from the poem.

1. All around her, the poet sees broken .... and pieces of .... that are burnt and black.
2. Mills produce yellow ....
3. When aircrafts fly, they give out .... from fuels.
4. The food that we eat is full of .... chemicals.

B. Read the lines from the poem and choose the correct option.

1. *Pouring of concrete and tearing out trees*
   This line suggests that humans
   a. cut down trees and make buildings in that place.
   b. do not make roads and buildings and do not cut trees.
   c. plant trees and put concrete around them to protect the plants.
2. *All sea life destined to a slow awful doom*
   This line means that
   a. life in the sea is better than life on land.
   b. the creatures living in the sea are flourishing.
   c. the creatures living in the sea are slowly dying out.
3. *Weapons of destruction tested at desolate sites*
   This line refers to
   a. armies fighting with a lot of weapons.
   b. wars taking place at faraway places.
   c. nuclear weapons being tested at remote places.

C. Answer the questions.

1. The first three stanzas of the poem talk about three types of pollution. What are they?
2. The poet ends each of the first three stanzas with a question. Why do you think she does so?

Life Skills and Values

Protecting the environment

1. What are the different kinds of pollution? Which ones are affecting you personally? How can you prevent pollution in your own way? Give ideas.
2. These days there is a lot of talk about pollution. Does it bother you? Do you think people just talk about pollution or is something being done to reduce it? Discuss.

VOCABULARY

Imagery

- **Imagery** is the use of visually descriptive language used in literary works, such as poems.
- Poets often use words in such a way that we can almost *see, hear* and even *smell* the things they describe. This produces rich mental pictures in the mind of a reader.
- Imagery also beautifies a piece of literature.

Read the first three stanzas of the poem. List out the things that you can *see, hear,* or *smell.*

1. What can one see? ....

....

....

....

2. What can one hear? ....

....

....

....

3. What can one smell? ....

....

....

....

ACTIVITY

Biodegradable and non-biodegradable wastes

- Waste consists of two types of materials – biodegradable and non-biodegradable.
- Biodegradable materials break down naturally. They rot or decompose with the help of bacteria or other living organisms. So, they are not dangerous to the environment. For example:

  dead or dried leaves, paper, used tea bags, vegetable peels
- Non-biodegradable materials do not break down and are dangerous to the environment. For example:

  plastic bags and straws, styrofoam cups
- There are different-coloured dustbins for throwing in each type of waste. If your locality doesn't have them, make sure you get them installed with the help of your parents and other adults.

A. You know that some materials biodegrade much more quickly than others. Study the decomposing timeline of these ten items. This will help you make more environmentally-friendly choices in your daily lives.

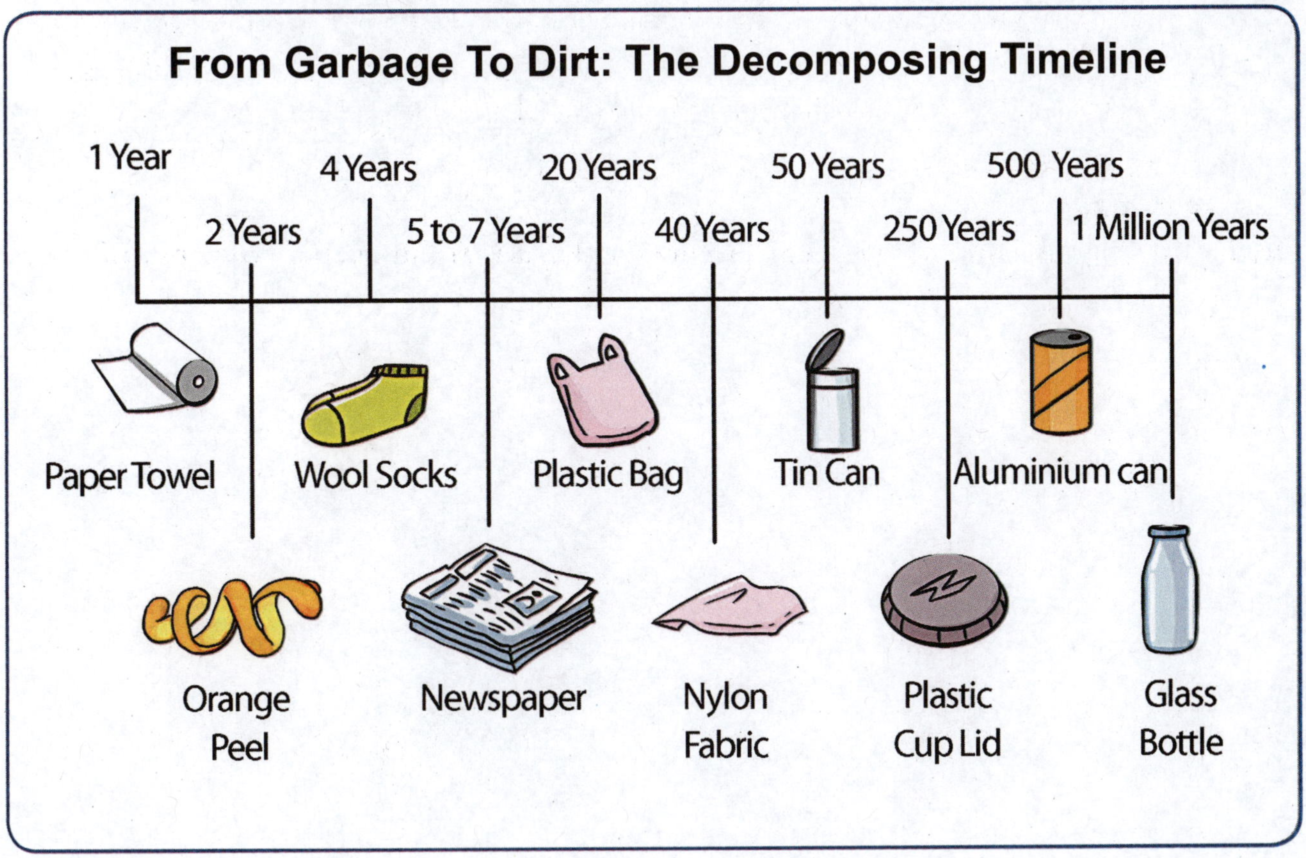

B. Work in pairs to find out about biodegradable and non-biodegradable wastes.

- Wear gloves, cover your nose and mouth with a cloth or mask, and go through the contents of your dustbin under the observation of adults.
- List all the items you find in it.
- Then sort out the biodegradable and non-biodegradable items.
- You can take the help of the Internet.
- Now put each item that you have found in the correct dustbin, and also list them out here.

PROJECT 2

Sacred Groves of India

Rivers, mountains and trees have always been worshipped in India. This worship is directly related to conservation of nature.

From pre-Vedic times, Indians have declared certain forest areas as sacred groves. These groves are dedicated to a certain god who looks after all the living creatures in that area. No one is allowed to hunt, cut down trees, or harm any form of life in the area. Even breaking a branch off a tree is not permitted.

Let us find out more about sacred groves and why they are important. You will need to consult books from the library and/or surf the Internet.

1. Find out names and location of five sacred groves of India and mark them on a map of India.
2. Now choose any one grove and study about it in detail.
   a. What is the exact location of the grove?
   b. What is the landform of the area—hill, coast, desert, plain?
   c. Which god is it dedicated to?
   d. What kind of plants, insects, birds and animals are found there? Name three of each.
   e. How does the grove help in the conservation of the natural environment in that area?

8 Thunder and Anansi

Myths in World Culture

OBJECTIVES

In this chapter, we will:

- *read an African folktale about a trickster.*
- *learn about synonyms and antonyms.*
- *learn the subject-verb-object structure, and the use of for and since.*
- *listen to a conversation and fill in the blanks.*
- *talk about reusing everyday items.*
- *learn to pronounce words with the silent letters b, l, r and s.*
- *write a recipe.*

WARM-UP

Mindfulness Activity
Be a superhero!

A. **Anansi, a character from African folktales, would often take the form of a spider. We all love Spider-Man. Spider-Man climbs up walls in a special way when he goes to help people.**

Let's take up the pose of Spider-Man, not on a wall but on the floor. Turn on all your senses, as Spider-Man would. Now see, hear, smell, and feel. Remain in this fully focused position for a minute or two. Then grab a piece of paper and write all you saw, heard, smelt and felt, and pin your paper on the noticeboard. Was your experience the same as your friends or different?

B. What does the word *culture* refer to? Study the chart and fill in the blank boxes with different aspects of culture.

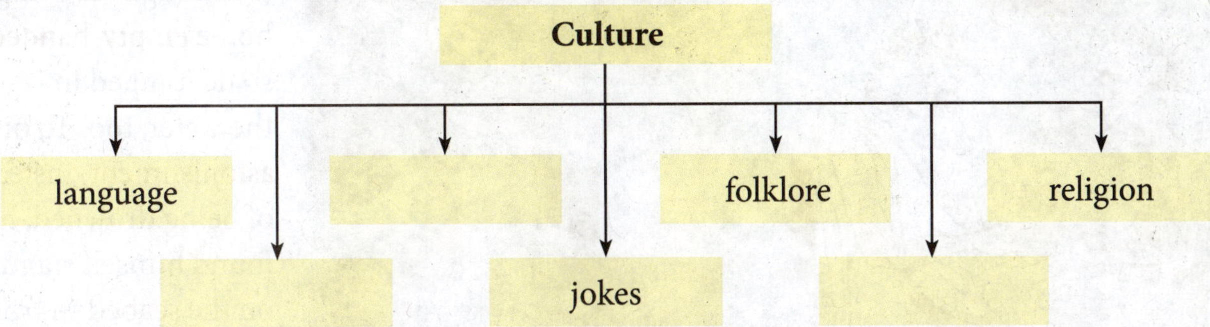

C. Folktales are stories with morals. They are passed on orally from one generation to the next. Folktales vary from region to region, and form an integral part of culture. Work in pairs and tell a folktale from your region.

READING

Anansi is a popular character and a great trickster in several West African folktales. The word 'anansi' means 'spider' in Twi, the language of Ghana, a west-African country. This is because in some stories, Anansi can change himself into a spider. Read this story where he tries to trick his family, although without disguising as a spider.

There had been a long and severe famine in the land where Anansi lived. He had been unable to obtain food for his poor family. One day, gazing out to sea, he saw a tiny island with a tall palm tree on it. He determined to reach the tree and pluck nuts from it. But he did not know how to get there.

When Anansi reached the beach, he saw an old broken boat. It did not look very strong, but Anansi decided to try it. His first six attempts were unsuccessful. However, the seventh time, he was successful. He rowed the old boat to the island and reached the palm tree.

Having tied the boat to the trunk of the tree, he climbed towards the nuts. Plucking all he could reach, he dropped them down into the boat. Alas, every one missed the boat and fell into the water, until only the last one remained. This he aimed even more carefully than the others, but it also fell into the water! He had not tasted even one and now all were gone.

Earth Speak

- Many countries around the world are hit by famines. A famine may be caused by drought, crop failure, overpopulation, etc.
- Famines result in widespread starvation, malnutrition, and even deaths.
- Palm trees grow in hot climates. There are over 2000 varieties of palm trees.
- The fruit of two palms, the date palm and the coconut palm, is consumed throughout the world.

trickster: a person who tricks or cheats people
famine: extreme scarcity of food
obtain: to get something by making an effort
island: a piece of land completely surrounded by water

Anansi could not bear the thought of going home empty-handed, so he jumped into the water, too. To his astonishment, instead of being drowned, he found himself standing on the seabed in front of a little cottage. From the cottage emerged an old man. He asked Anansi what he wanted so badly that he had come to Thunder's cottage to get it. Anansi told him his sad story. Thunder was most sympathetic. He went into the cottage and brought a cooking pot. He presented it to Anansi, telling him that he would never be hungry again. The pot would always supply enough food for him and his family. Anansi was most grateful. He left Thunder with many thanks.

Anxious to test the pot, Anansi only waited till he was in the old boat again and said, 'Pot, pot, what you used to do for your master, do now for me.' Immediately, tasty food appeared in the pot! Anansi enjoyed a hearty meal.

When he reached land again, he wanted to run home and give all his family a good meal. But a selfish, greedy fear stopped him. *What if I should use up all the magic of the pot on them and have nothing more left for myself? I had better keep the pot a secret so that I can enjoy a meal whenever I want to.* So, he hid the pot.

Anansi reached home pretending to be tired and hungry. But there was not a grain of food in the house. His wife and poor children were very hungry, but selfish Anansi paid no attention to that. He congratulated himself at the thought of his magic pot, now safely hidden in his room. Whenever he felt hungry, he went to his room and enjoyed a good meal.

empty-handed: without getting what you wanted
astonishment: a feeling of very great surprise
seabed: the floor of the sea/ocean
emerged: came out (of a dark, confined, or hidden place)
sympathetic: kind to somebody who is hurt or sad; showing that you understand and care about others' problems
grateful: feeling or showing an appreciation because somebody has done something kind for you or has done as you asked
anxious: nervous about something which may or may not happen
hearty meal: a large meal making you feel full
pretending: behaving in a particular way to make others believe something that is not true

Anansi's family became weak and got thinner and thinner, but he grew plumper by the day. They began to suspect that Anansi was eating something nutritious secretly without sharing that with them. They decided to find it out.

Anansi's eldest son, Kweku Tsin, had the power of changing himself into any form he chose. He changed himself into a tiny fly and accompanied his father everywhere. One day, Anansi entered his room and closed the door. Kweku Tsin managed to slip inside. He saw Anansi take the pot and have a fine meal. Having placed the pot back in its hiding place after the meal, Anansi went out.

As soon as Anansi was out of sight, Kweku Tsin took out the pot, ordered it to prepare food, and called all his hungry family. They enjoyed a tasty, filling meal. When they had finished, Anansi's wife said that she would take the pot to the village and give everybody a meal.

This she did, but alas, in preparing so much food at one time, the pot grew too hot and melted away. What was to be done now? Anansi would be very angry. His wife forbade everyone to mention the pot.

Anansi returned home, and as usual went into his room. He searched for the pot but it was not there. *Someone must have discovered it*, he thought. He suspected his family to be the culprits and decided to punish them. But he said nothing to anyone about the matter and waited till morning.

As soon as it was morning, he started off for the shore, where the old boat lay. He got into the boat, which started of its own accord and took him to the palm tree. Anansi tied the boat to the tree and climbed the tree. This time when he aimed the nuts at the boat, they fell into it. He got down, threw the nuts into the water, and jumped after them.

Again, he found himself in front of Thunder's cottage. He told his story to Thunder, and Thunder seemed to show the same sympathy. This time he presented Anansi with a stick. Anansi was very eager to try the magic properties of his new gift, so he swam back to his boat very fast.

plumper: slightly fatter
suspect: to have an idea that something is probably true but without having definite proof
accompanied: went with
out of sight: not visible any more
forbade: ordered not to do something
culprits: persons who have done something wrong or against the law
of its own accord: without being asked, forced, or helped; by itself

ashore: towards or onto land, having come from an area of water such as the sea or a river
bruises: blue, brown or purple marks that appear on the skin after somebody has fallen or been hit

'Stick, stick,' Anansi said, 'do for me what you used to do for your master.' As soon as Anansi said that, the stick began to beat him so severely that he had to jump into the water and swim ashore, leaving the boat and the stick to drift away. He returned home complaining about his bruises and wishing he had acted more wisely from the beginning.

SUMMARY

During a famine, Anansi, a trickster found a tall palm tree with nuts on an island. He plucked and threw the nuts in the boat but they fell in the water. He jumped into the sea, and to his surprise, saw a cottage. It was the home of Thunder. On hearing Anansi's story, Thunder gave him a magic pot which would give him food whenever he wanted. Anansi kept the pot for himself and grew plump, while his family starved. Suspecting something, his family followed him and found his secret. Soon after, his wife took the pot to feed the whole village, but the pot melted away. When Anansi went to the island again, Thunder gave him a magic stick that beat him black and blue. Anansi learnt his lesson.

COMPREHENSION

A. Choose the correct option.

1. Anansi could not get food for his family because
   a. the market was very far off.
   b. there was a famine in the land.
   c. he was too lazy to earn money.
2. To feed his family, Anansi determined to get
   a. a well-paying job.
   b. food from the market despite the difficulty.
   c. a few nuts from a palm tree growing on an island.
3. Anansi was able to pluck a lot of nuts from the palm tree but
   a. they fell into the sea.
   b. they rolled far away.
   c. they were all spoilt.

4. Anansi learnt a lesson
    a. while enjoying a good meal.
    b. when the magic pot was stolen.
    c. when the magic stick beat him severely.

B. Read the sentences and number them in the correct order.

1. The cooking pot was magical and produced tasty food. ☐
2. He did not drown; he reached an underwater cottage. ☐
3. After hearing Anansi's sad story, Thunder gave him a cooking pot. ☐
4. When all the nuts fell into the water, Anansi also jumped into the water. ☐
5. Anansi became plumper while his family grew thinner due to lack of food. ☐
6. The cottage belonged to Thunder, who asked Anansi what the matter was. ☐
7. His family began to wonder why Anansi was not growing thinner like them. ☐
8. Selfish and greedy Anansi did not show the pot to his family but hid it in his room. ☐

C. Answer the questions.

1. Why did Anansi travel in a broken boat?
2. Why did Anansi jump into the water after having failed to get the nuts in the boat?
3. Why did Anansi keep getting plumper?
4. When Anansi reached the palm tree the second time, the nuts he dropped fell into the boat. Instead of taking them back to his family, he threw the nuts into the water. Did he do the right thing? Justify your answer.
5. Why do you think Thunder gave a stick to Anansi the second time?
6. The character of Anansi changes as the story progresses. How?
7. Imagine you are Kweku Tsin. Explain how you felt when you found out the secret of your father getting plumper.
8. Imagine Thunder gave Anansi a robe that made him invisible, instead of the stick. Write a different ending for the story keeping this in mind.

Life Skills and Values — **Making a difference**

1. Anansi's wife decided to take the pot to the village and provide a meal to all the villagers. What does this tell you about her? How else could she have used the pot? Share your ideas.
2. Each one of us has a quality that we can use for the good of people around us. Think of ways in which you can do something to create a difference. Discuss.

VOCABULARY

Synonyms and antonyms

- A **synonym** is a word which means the same or nearly the same as another word. For example:

  good – nice *right – correct*

- An **antonym** is a word which means the opposite of another word. For example:

  good – bad *right – wrong*

A. Fill in the crossword.

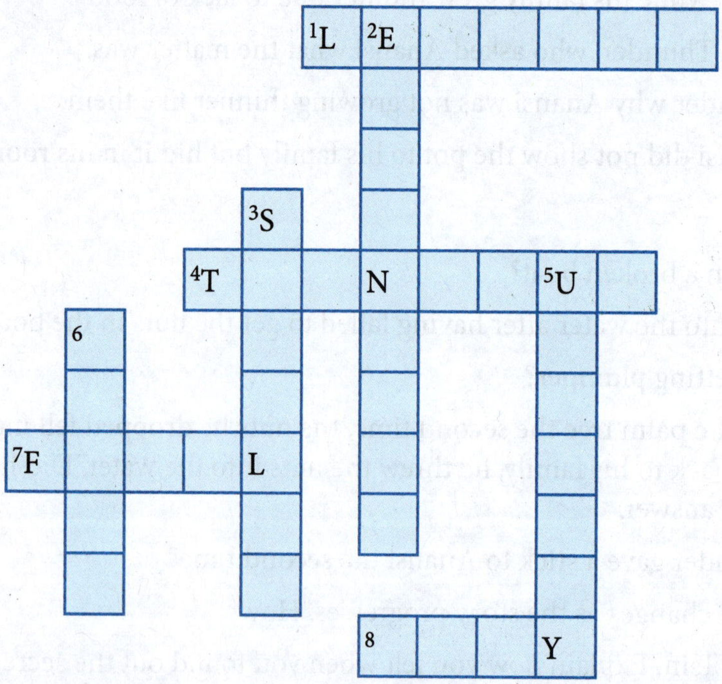

Across

1. synonym of *long*
4. synonym of *grateful*
7. synonym of *last*
8. antonym of *few*

Down

2. antonym of *cheap*
3. antonym of *deep*
5. synonym of *sad*
6. antonym of *noisy*

B. Fill in the blanks with the antonyms of the words given in the box.

big *cheap* *cloudy* *far-off* *few* *hot* *quiet* *wet*

On a .... day, a little girl went to a park. There were .... people in the park and it was .... She sat on the .... grass and took out a .... bottle of water from her basket. She drank the water and put the bottle back. She saw a woman with a .... can of juice in her hands. She also wanted to have juice and went to the .... stall. The juice was ...., so she didn't buy it.

GRAMMAR

Subject-verb-object structure

- A **sentence** is a group of words that contains a subject and a verb. It expresses a complete idea.
- The most basic sentence structure in the English language is:

  subject + verb + object
- The *action* word is the verb.
- Whoever/Whatever performs an action is the **subject** of a sentence. To find out the subject of the sentence, put 'who' or 'what' before the verb. The answer is the subject.
- Whoever/Whatever receives the action is the **object** of the sentence. To find out the object of the sentence, put 'what' after the verb. The answer is the object.

  Read the sentences.

  Anansi rowed the boat.
  Anansi plucked the nuts.
  Anansi hid the cooking pot.

  In the three sentences, *rowed, plucked,* and *hid* are verbs.

  Who rowed/plucked/hid?

  Anansi (doer of the action)

  So *Anansi* is the subject.

  Anansi rowed/plucked/hid what?

  Boat/nut/cooking pot (receiver of the action). They are objects.

A. Identify the subject, verb, and object in each sentence.

1. I read a story last night.
   a. Subject: .... b. Verb: .... c. Object: ....
2. The young boy played the piano.
   a. Subject: .... b. Verb: .... c. Object: ....
3. My mother baked a cake yesterday.
   a. Subject: .... b. Verb: .... c. Object: ....
4. Sameer likes history very much.
   a. Subject: .... b. Verb: .... c. Object: ....
5. She designs clothes beautifully.
   a. Subject: .... b. Verb: .... c. Object: ....
6. I accidentally tore my T-shirt.
   a. Subject: .... b. Verb: .... c. Object: ....

B. Use the words in the table to make as many sentences as possible. Underline the subjects, verbs, and objects separately in your sentences. Write S, V, and O under them respectively. One has been done for you.

We ate pizza.
S V O

We		ate	a car
They	is/are	built	pizza
Varun	was/were	forgot	cricket
The dog		played	waffles
The children		riding	the wall
My neighbours		studying	the books
My sister and I		guarding	the house

for and *since*

- We use *for* and *since* to talk about time.
- We use *for* when we talk about a period of time—how long an activity lasts.

  The school will be shut for two months.

  They have been living in the hills for three years.
- We use *since* when we talk about the starting time of an action or event—when something began.

  The children have been shouting slogans since 9 a.m.

  The water in the river has been rising since March.

***for* + a period of time**	***since* + a point in time (till now)**
when we measure how long something lasts	when we know when something started in the past
The action/event has a start point and an end point.	The action/event has a start point and continues in the present.

C. Complete the phrases with *for* or *since*.

1. .... July
2. .... ten years
3. .... the last month
4. .... we moved here
5. .... the day I left Delhi

D. Fill in the blanks with *for* or *since*.

1. He has been planting trees .... January 2017.
2. The boys have been watching the film.................... 2 p.m.
3. She worked on the project to save water .... three years.
4. Tara has been studying .... 9 o'clock.
5. Gauri, the village council leader, spoke to the villagers .... an hour.

LISTENING AND SPEAKING

Listening

A. Listen to the conversation between the children and fill in the blanks.

1. Anansi is an .... character from the country of ....
2. The .... people were the first to start telling stories about Anansi.
3. Anansi is a .... cum ....
4. Anansi is also known as ...., ..., and ....
5. In the US, he is known as ....
6. All his stories have a ....; they teach a lesson.
7. According to one story, Anansi filled a .... with wisdom and tried to hide it in a ....
8. However, the .... dropped and all the wisdom fell out.
9. It was carried to all parts of the .... by the wind and the ....
10. ...., ..., and .... games have been made on Anansi stories.

Speaking

B. Work in pairs. Identify an item of everyday use, such as a newspaper. Think of at least four different ways in which the item may be reused. Share your ways with the class. You may follow the examples given below.

Newspaper

- Place crumpled newspaper in wet shoes to dry them off.
- Use newspapers to clean glass tabletops, mirrors, and crockery.
- Cover unripe fruit with newspaper for a couple of days to ripen it.

Pronunciation

Silent letters *b*, *l*, *r* and *s*

- A silent letter in a word is a letter that is not pronounced.
- About sixty per cent of English words have silent letters.
- The letter **b** is silent when it comes
  - after *m* at the end of a word. For example:
    lamb *limb*
  - before *t* at the end of a word. For example:
    debt
- The letter **l** is usually silent when it comes just before *m* and *k*. For example:
  calm *folk*
- The letter **r** is silent when it comes before a consonant or at the end of a word. For example:
  garden *hear*
- The letter **s** is sometimes silent when it comes before *l*. For example:
  island *aisle*

C. Write the silent letter in the box.

1. butter ☐
2. chalk ☐
3. doubt ☐
4. dumb ☐
5. half ☐
6. isle ☐
7. Norway ☐
8. plumber ☐
9. purple ☐
10. walk ☐

D. Choose the correct option.

1. The letter **b** is silent in
   a. comb. b. bat. c. business.
2. The letter **l** is silent in
   a. tall. b. slim. c. calf.
3. The letter **r** is silent in
   a. storm. b. great. c. wearing.
4. The letter **s** is silent in
   a. psychologist. b. moist. c. aisle.

WRITING

Describing a procedure

Anansi did not need to cook. All he had to do was to order the magic pot to cook! But in real life, we must follow a procedure or a recipe to prepare a dish. Describe the procedure/recipe for making a sandwich with your favourite filling.

You may begin like this:

- Take four slices of bread.
- Spread butter...

9 The Wizard of Oz

Travel and Adventure

OBJECTIVES

In this chapter, we will:

- *read a play based on the popular American novel The Wizard of Oz.*
- *learn French words used in English.*
- *learn the use of direct and reported speech, reporting verbs, and inverted commas.*
- *listen to the description of a character and complete information.*
- *talk about reducing the impact of natural disasters and learn the different pronunciations of ch.*
- *create a comic strip.*

WARM-UP

Mindfulness Activity
Travelling in mind

A. Don't we all love to travel? Let's travel while we are in class. Impossible! Not really. Take a blank sheet of paper and draw a place you would like to go to—a forest, a beach or a hill station.

Take a good look at your drawing. Now close your eyes and 'travel' to that place. 'Look' around you. Try to 'hear' and 'smell' all that is nearby—trees/sea/mountains. How do you feel when you are there? Does it bring a smile to your face?

B. The word *travel* comes from the old French word *travaillier*. Find these travel-related words in the word grid.

cruise *expedition*
excursion *light*
globetrotting *journey*
pilgrimage *trek*
tour *voyage*

a	x	t	i	v	b	r	k	m	o
o	j	o	u	r	n	e	y	h	b
t	b	u	r	d	g	s	z	f	p
x	p	r	e	q	f	t	i	g	k
m	b	i	z	c	l	v	k	l	o
e	x	p	e	d	i	t	i	o	n
k	l	t	x	c	g	g	f	b	b
t	y	v	c	s	h	j	g	e	f
r	g	m	u	o	t	u	k	t	w
e	w	c	r	u	i	s	e	r	t
k	j	z	s	l	w	j	q	o	i
a	s	p	i	x	h	s	a	t	u
g	y	v	o	y	a	g	e	t	o
d	v	k	n	s	e	i	g	i	w
l	o	w	h	k	u	t	v	n	m
p	i	l	g	r	i	m	a	g	e

READING

A little girl, Dorothy, gets lost in a strange land. Let's read how she faces unfamiliar and difficult situations there.

Characters

- Narrator
- Toto, Dorothy's dog
- Scarecrow
- Lion
- Wicked Witch of the West
- Good Witch of the South
- Dorothy, a little girl
- Good Witch of the North
- Tin Man
- Wizard of Oz
- Winged Monkeys

Earth Speak

- Kansas is a state in the United States of America. It is covered by prairies.
- Prairies are vast stretches of grasslands. They are suitable for agriculture.
- A tornado is a violent storm with strong circular winds. It can be very dangerous as it can break apart buildings, knock down trees, and even toss cars into the air.
- Tornadoes look like funnels or wedges.

Narrator: Dorothy lived with her Uncle and Aunt in the Kansas prairies. One day Dorothy and her dog, Toto, were playing inside the house when a large tornado appeared. It picked the house right up off its foundation with Dorothy and Toto still inside! It carried them high into the sky. After several miles, the house landed with a crash.

SCENE 1

Narrator: After the crash, Dorothy walks to the door and finds herself in a strange land. Standing before her is a crowd of tiny people, called the Munchkins. The Munchkins seem very happy to see Dorothy.

Dorothy: Who are you?

Good Witch of the North: I'm the Witch of the North. We'd like to thank you for killing the Wicked Witch of the East.

Dorothy: What do you mean? I haven't killed anyone.

Good Witch of the North: (*pointing to the corner of the house*) Look there! Can you see those two feet in silver shoes sticking out? Your house landed on top of the Wicked Witch of the East. We had been the Witch's slaves for years. Today, you have rid us of the Witch and we are free!

(*handing over the silver shoes*) Here, take these silver shoes of the Wicked Witch of the East. They are yours now; they're magical.

emerald: a bright green precious stone; here used as a proper noun, as the name of a city
scarecrow: a figure made to look like a person, that is dressed in old clothes and put in a field to frighten birds away

Dorothy: Oh, thank you so much! The shoes fit me perfectly. (*after a pause*) Does anyone know how I can get back to Kansas?

(*Everyone shakes their head.*)

Good Witch of the North: We haven't heard of Kansas. But, maybe, the Wizard of Oz can help you. He lives in the Emerald City.

Dorothy: How can I reach the Emerald City?

Good Witch of the North: Follow, follow, follow the Yellow Brick Road.

Narrator: The little Munchkins lead Dorothy to the Yellow Brick Road. She waves good-bye and skips down the road with Toto.

SCENE 2

Narrator: After a while, Dorothy reaches a cornfield and stops to rest. Close by on a pole is a scarecrow put there to frighten away the birds.

Scarecrow: Hello!

Dorothy: (*surprised*) Did you speak?

Scarecrow: Yes, how do you do? And who are you?

Dorothy: I am Dorothy, and this is my dog, Toto. We are from Kansas. We are going to meet the Wizard of Oz.

Scarecrow: I am a scarecrow. I have been stuffed with straw and have no brains. I do wish I had some.

Dorothy: Would you like to come with us?

Scarecrow: Yes. *(Dorothy helps him climb down the pole.)* Let's go.

Narrator: The Scarecrow comes down and they go off together.

SCENE 3

Narrator: Soon Dorothy and the Scarecrow come to a patch of trees where they hear a noise. In the middle of the trees is a man made of tin. He stands **motionless** with an axe in his hand.

Dorothy: Did you say something?

Tin Man: Yes. Please bring me some oil!

Narrator: Dorothy finds some oil and oils the Tin Man from head to toe.

Tin Man: Thank you. I had been out **chopping** down trees some time ago when it suddenly started to rain. Before I could get out of the rain, I was **rusted** badly and could barely move. I'd have stayed here forever if you hadn't come along. Say, why are you here?

Dorothy: We are going to meet the Wizard of Oz.

Tin Man: (*looking curious*) Do you think the Wizard could give me a heart?

Scarecrow: Maybe, he can. Would you like to join us?

Tin Man: Yes, I will come with you.

Narrator: Dorothy, the Scarecrow, and the Tin Man set off together and travel for many miles.

SCENE 4

Narrator: The travellers now reach a thick forest. Suddenly, a fierce lion leaps onto the path with a loud roar. He pushes the Scarecrow and then jumps on the Tin Man. As the beast opens his mouth, Dorothy rushes forward and punches the lion on the nose!

motionless: not moving; still
chopping: cutting into pieces
rusted: covered in a reddish-brown substance called rust

Dorothy: You big beast, you ought to be ashamed of yourself. You're nothing but a big coward.

Lion: (*rubbing his nose and almost crying*) I know I'm a coward, but I can't help it.

Dorothy: Oh, I am sorry! Please don't cry. I just can't understand how a lion like you is a coward.

Lion: I was born that way; I wish to have courage so I could be the King of Beasts.

Dorothy: Come with us to the Wizard of Oz. I'm sure the Wizard will give you courage.

Dorothy, the Scarecrow, the Tin Man, and the Lion: Oh, we're off to see the Wizard, the Wonderful Wizard of Oz.

palace: the official home of a king, queen or ruler
robe: a long loose outer piece of clothing, especially one worn as a sign of rank at a special ceremony
throne: a special chair used by a king or queen to sit on during ceremonies

SCENE 5

Narrator: At long last, the travellers come to the Emerald City. It is the most beautiful place that any of them has ever seen. Dorothy and her friends come to the palace of the great Wizard of Oz. They walk up to the guard at the door and ask for the Wizard. The guard leads them to a large room. The Wizard is dressed in a long green robe and is seated on a marble throne.

Wizard of Oz: I am Oz, the Great Wizard. Welcome! What brings you here?

Dorothy: I want to go back home to Kansas.

The Scarecrow: I'd like some brains.

The Tin Man: I need a heart.

The Lion: I want courage.

Wizard of Oz: (*with a serious face*) I can help you only if you bring me the broomstick of the Wicked Witch of the West.

Dorothy: Oh! So we will have to travel once again!
(*to the others*) Let's go!

Narrator: The Guard gives the travellers directions to find the Wicked Witch of the West. They run as fast as they can.

SCENE 6

Narrator: After some time, Dorothy, the Lion, and Toto feel very tired and decide to rest. They lie down on the soft grass and, in no time at all, fall fast asleep while the Tin Man and the Scarecrow stand guard. The Wicked Witch of the West spots them from afar with her magical powers.

Wicked Witch of the West: Who's that girl with silver shoes? She has four friends with her. I have only one eye but it's as powerful as a telescope! Let me use my magical Golden Cap and summon my slaves, the Winged Monkeys.

(*to the Winged Monkeys*) Go and get that girl with the silver shoes! And capture her friends too!

Narrator: The Winged Monkeys capture Dorothy and her friends and bring them to the Wicked Witch of the West.

Wicked Witch of the West: (*to Dorothy*) Give me those shoes!

Dorothy: No! They're mine! The Good Witch of the North gave me these shoes!

Narrator: The Wicked Witch of the West tries to get the shoes off but she can't. They are magic shoes and can only be removed if Dorothy wishes so.

broomstick: a broom with a long handle and small thin sticks at the end, or the handle of a broom
spots: sees or notices, especially suddenly or when it is not easy to do so
from afar: from a distance
summon: to order someone to come to you
capture: to catch somebody and keep him/her as a prisoner

Wicked Witch of the West: If you don't give me your shoes, I'll kill your dog.

Narrator: The Witch reaches for Toto, who bites her hand.

Wicked Witch of the West: Ouch! You'll pay for this, you bad dog!

Narrator: Dorothy sees a pail of water nearby, grabs it, and throws the water on the Wicked Witch of the West. Instantly, the Wicked Witch gives a loud cry and begins to melt. Soon she disappears. The Winkies, the creatures of the land, are happy because they are free from the Wicked Witch's spell.

Dorothy: Look! The Wicked Witch's broom is on the floor! Let's take it to the Wizard!

Narrator: Dorothy takes the Golden Cap and orders the Winged Monkeys to take them back to the Wizard of Oz.

SCENE 7

Narrator: Dorothy and her friends return to the Wizard.

Wizard: I'm happy to see you. Do you have the Witch's broom?

Dorothy: Yes, great Wizard. Not only do we have the broom, we've also killed the Wicked Witch.

rejoicing: expressing great happiness about something

Narrator: The news of the Wicked Witch's death spreads throughout the Emerald City and there is great rejoicing.

Dorothy: (*to the Wizard*) Now, will you help us, please?

Wizard of Oz: I am sorry but I am not a wizard. I am just an ordinary old man. But wait, I can do something. Scarecrow, I am filling your head with pins and needles. This will make you sharp. Tin Man, I am placing this heart-shaped clock inside you. Now, you have a heart. Lion, take this saucer and drink the foul-tasting green liquid in it. You are brave to drink that. It's what I call real courage. Dorothy, I can't help you. Why don't you go to the Good Witch of the South. She may be able to help you get back to Kansas.

Narrator: Dorothy and her friends set out once again to meet the Good Witch of the South.

SCENE 8

Narrator: The travellers reach the beautiful castle of the Good Witch of the South.

foul-tasting: having a very unpleasant taste
set out: to start (a journey)
castle: a large strong building with thick high walls and towers, built in the past by kings or queens to defend themselves against attack

Good Witch of the South: How can I help you?

Dorothy: I want to go back home, to Kansas.

Good Witch of the South: You could have gone back home a long time ago if you knew you had magic with you.

Dorothy: What do you mean?

Good Witch of the South: The silver shoes will take you home. All you need to do is click your heels together three times.

Dorothy: Really? I am so happy! I can finally go back home. (*to the Good Witch of the South*) Take this Golden Cap, and thank you for your help!

Come, Toto. (*clicking the heels of her shoes together three times*) Take me back to Kansas!

Good Witch of the South: Goodbye! Scarecrow, you will now rule over the Emerald City. Tin Man, you will rule over the Winkies. Lion, you will rule over the beasts in the forest.

Narrator: Soon, Dorothy is back home. She is happy to be back with her uncle and aunt but knows that she would never forget her wonderful adventures in the land of Oz.

SUMMARY

A tornado hit the house where Dorothy lived with her uncle and aunt in Kansas. She and her dog, Toto, were swept away to a strange land, the Land of the Munchkins. When her house dropped, it fell on the Wicked Witch of the East, killing her. The Munchkins were now free from the Witch. They gave Dorothy the magical shoes of the Witch and asked her to go to the Wizard of Oz to find her way back home. Moving on the Yellow Brick Road, she met a brainless Scarecrow, a heartless Tin Man and a cowardly Lion. They all went together to Emerald city of Oz to get what they wanted. When they met him, he asked them to bring the broomstick of the Wicked Witch of the West. Dorothy managed to defeat the Witch. In the end, everyone's wishes were fulfilled though in a manner they had not expected.

COMPREHENSION

A. Mark the sentences as true (T) or false (F).

1. Dorothy lived in Kansas with her parents. ☐
2. Toto was Dorothy's pet monkey. ☐
3. Dorothy's house was swept away in a flash flood. ☐
4. Dorothy's house finally settled in the Land of the Munchkins. ☐
5. The house landed on the Wicked Witch of the East and killed her. ☐

B. Read the sentences and number them in correct order.

1. Nobody knew where Kansas was. ☐
2. She presented Dorothy with the silver shoes of the witch. ☐
3. The Good Witch of the North welcomed Dorothy to her land. ☐
4. She asked the people how she could go back to her home in Kansas. ☐
5. She was advised to go to the Wizard of Oz in the Emerald City for help. ☐
6. On the way, she met the Scarecrow, the Tin Man, and the Lion, who also went with her. ☐
7. She was also advised that she could reach the Emerald City by following the Yellow Brick Road. ☐
8. When they met the Wizard, he asked them to bring the broom of the Wicked Witch of the West. ☐

C. Choose the correct option.

1. The Scarecrow wanted the Wizard
   a. to give him brains.
   b. to give him a heart.
   c. to give him a longer tail.
2. The Tin Man had rusted because
   a. he had fallen in a puddle.
   b. he had got wet in the rain.
   c. he had gone swimming in a river.

3. The Lion was
   a. a coward and wanted courage.
   b. very brave and wanted some weapons.
   c. very strong and wanted to learn martial arts.

D. Answer the questions.

1. What did the Wicked Witch of the West want Dorothy to give her? Why?
2. What did the Wizard give to the Scarecrow, the Tin Man, and the Lion? Did he really help them? Explain.
3. *You could have gone back home a long time ago if you knew you had magic with you.* Who is speaking to whom here? What magic is being referred to?
4. The Scarecrow wanted brains, the Tin Man wanted a heart, and the Lion wanted courage. If you were given a choice, what would you ask for? Give reasons for your choice.
5. How do you think Dorothy felt when she reached home?

Life Skills and Values — Patience and travel

1. Dorothy was a brave and patient girl. Do you agree? Why/Why not? Discuss.
2. Talk about a time when you travelled to a new place with your parents. How was this place different from your hometown/city? What were the challenges for you in the new place? What did you learn because it was a new experience? Share your thoughts.

VOCABULARY

French words in English

- There are many words used in English that originated in other languages but are now considered a part of English vocabulary. For example:

  Café is originally a French word.

- Here are a few more French words and their meanings.

  adieu: goodbye

  bon voyage: happy journey

  boutique: a small shop that sells fashionable clothes or expensive gifts

  chic: stylish

  crèche: a place where young children are cared for while their parents are working, shopping, studying, etc.

  décor: the style in which the inside of a building is decorated

  restaurant: a place where you can buy and eat a meal

Write sentences using any three words of French origin you just learned.

1. ....

2. ....

3. ....

GRAMMAR

Direct Speech and Reported Speech

- We can report the words of a speaker in two ways.
- They are direct speech and reported speech.

Direct speech

- Reporting the exact words of a speaker as spoken by the speaker is called **direct speech**.
- The exact words of the speaker are put within inverted commas ('...').

Dorothy said to the Good Witch, *'I haven't killed anyone.'*

'Your house landed on top of the Wicked Witch,' replied the Good Witch.

Reported speech

- Reporting what somebody said in our own words, without using the speaker's exact words, is called **reported speech** or **indirect speech**.

Dorothy told the Good Witch *that she hadn't killed anyone.*

The Good Witch replied *that her house had landed on top of the Wicked Witch.*

Rules for changing direct speech into reported speech

We make the following changes when we change direct speech into reported speech:

- The inverted commas are removed.
- Changes are made in the pronouns.
- A reporting verb, such as *said, told, asked,* is used.
- Changes are made in the tense of the verb if the reporting verb is in the past tense.

A. Identify whether the sentences are in direct speech (D) or reported speech (R).

1. The Good Witch of the North told Dorothy that the silver shoes were magical. ☐
2. Dorothy asked the Scarecrow, 'Did you speak?' ☐
3. The Scarecrow said, 'I have been stuffed with straw and have no brains.' ☐
4. The Tin Man said, 'Please bring me some oil.' ☐
5. Dorothy exclaimed that it was a beautiful road. ☐

B. Change the sentences into reported speech.

1. The Lion said, 'I want courage.'

   ....

2. The Good Witch said, 'The Wizard of Oz can help you.'

   ....

3. The Good Witch of the South said to Dorothy, 'The silver shoes will take you home.'

   ....

4. The Wizard said to the Lion, 'You were brave to drink that.'

   ....

Reporting verbs

- When we report something in reported speech, we use a reporting verb.

  Dorothy told the Good Witch that she hadn't killed anyone.

  Here, *told* is a reporting verb.

- The use of a reporting verb depends on the meaning of the sentence. Some more examples of reporting verbs are *said, requested, replied, advised, asked,* and *enquired.*

  'Please give me a glass of milk,' said Dorothy to a Munchkin.

  Dorothy requested a Munchkin to give her a glass of milk.

  The Wizard said to Dorothy, 'You should fly back to Kansas.'

  The Wizard advised Dorothy to fly back to Kansas.

C. Choose the reporting verb to report each statement.

1. 'I'll send you a letter every day from Kansas.'

   a. insisted b. promised

2. 'If I were you, I'd go to the Wizard of Oz.'

   a. asked b. suggested

3. 'I'll guard you while you sleep, Dorothy.'

   a. offered b. requested

4. 'You should've told me about the shoes earlier.'

   a. announced b. complained

5. 'Welcome to our city, young girl.'

   a. greeted b. announced

Inverted commas

- Inverted commas ('...') are punctuation marks used to mark the beginning and end of direct speech.
- In direct speech, full stops/question marks/exclamation marks are put inside the inverted commas. For example:

  Dorothy said to the Scarecrow, 'Come with me to the Wizard.'
- They are also used to mark a word or a phrase being discussed or to show that it is being quoted from somewhere. In this case, the full stops/question marks/exclamation marks are put outside the inverted commas. For example:

  The professor spoke on 'The Impact of Cyclones'.

  In her own words, it is her 'most favourite book'.
- Names of articles, short stories, or poems are also put in inverted commas. For example:

  I loved the story 'Kabuliwallah'.
- Remember that American English usually uses double inverted commas ("...").

D. Insert inverted commas in the sentences, wherever necessary.

1. Sandra said, Have you seen the movie The Wizard of Oz?
2. Kanta said, It's raining outside. Shall we play carrom indoors?
3. Madhu said, What a beautiful rainbow!
4. I don't agree with you, said Kamal, I think my pen is better.
5. I have to write an essay on Means of Transport.
6. The board displayed the quote, A room without books is like a garden without flowers.

LISTENING AND SPEAKING

Listening

A. Listen to the description of a character in a play and fill in the blanks.

1. *The Tempest* is a play written by .... Shakespeare.
2. Prospero is the .... character in the story.
3. He is a .... duke.
4. He is engrossed in learning ....
5. He uses magic to .... others, create storms and provide entertainment to others.
6. He is a .... personality.

Speaking

Collaboration

B. Get in groups of five and brainstorm for ideas to reduce the impact of natural disasters.

Answer these questions with the help of the Internet and the library:

- What is a disaster?
- Are disasters caused by nature or by humans? Or by both?
- What are some natural disasters?

Now choose a natural disaster.

- Find out more about the natural disaster.
- How does it affect our lives?
- Can the problems be reduced? In what ways?

Create a mind map based on your research and tell your class about your findings.

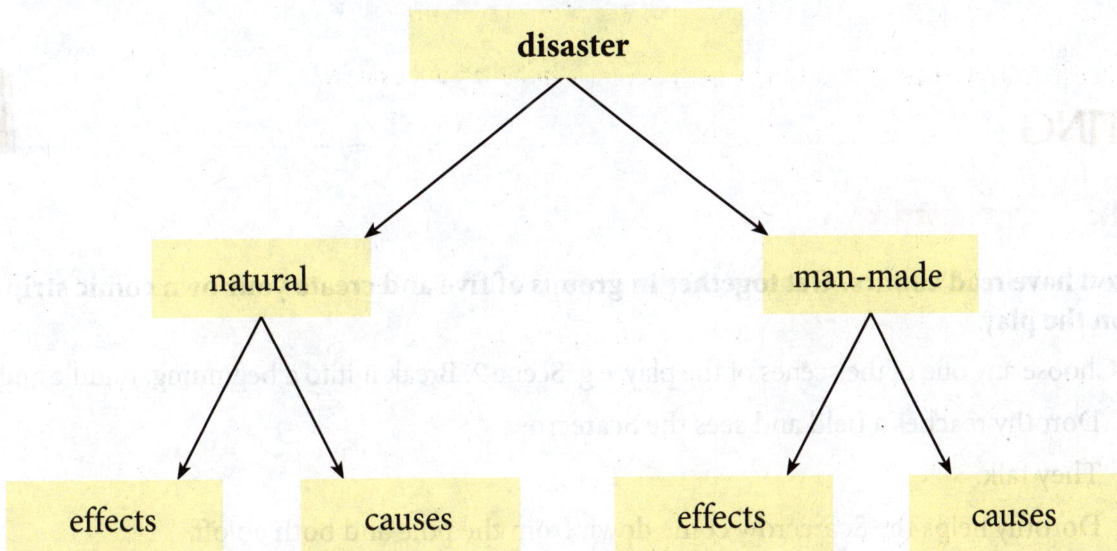

Pronunciation

Pronunciation of *ch*

- The letter combination **ch** is pronounced in three different ways.
- In most words, **ch** has the /ch/ sound. For example:

  chase, chicken, choose, church, much, rich
- In words borrowed from French, **ch** has the /sh/ sound. For example:

  chauffeur, chef, machine, moustache
- In words borrowed from Greek, **ch** has the /k/ sound. For example:

  ache, character, chemist, choir, school

C. Identify the sound of *ch* in the following words and place them in the correct boxes.

anchor *architect* *brochure* *chair* *charade* *chocolate*
chop *chord* *Christmas* *chin* *crochet* *parachute*

/ch/ sound	/sh/ sound	/k/ sound
1.	1.	1. ....
2.	2.	2. ....
3.	3.	3. ....
4.	4.	4. ....

WRITING

Creating a comic strip

All of you have read comics. Get together in groups of five and create your own comic strip based on the play.

Step 1: Choose any one of the scenes of the play, e.g. Scene 2. Break it into a beginning, middle and end.

- Dorothy reaches a field and sees the Scarecrow.
- They talk.
- Dorothy helps the Scarecrow come down from the pole and both go off.

Step 2: Draw four frames (boxes) on a rectangular sheet.

Step 3: Draw the two characters in very basic shapes or stick figures using a pencil.

E.g. The first frame will show the Scarecrow on a pole and Dorothy standing nearby.

Step 4: Add narration on the top.

E.g. Dorothy reaches a cornfield.

Step 5: Add speech bubbles.

E.g. In the first frame: Scarecrow – *Hello!* Dorothy – *Did you speak?*

Step 6: Draw the background.

E.g. Cornfields in the first frame

Step 7: Colour the drawings.

Your comic strip is ready! Wasn't that easy?

Remember to assign a task to each member in the group.

A: dialogue writing

B: drawing frames and characters

C: colouring and fact-checking from the play

D: final editing

E: presenting

Does the first frame of your comic strip look like this?

Dorothy reaches a cornfield.

Frame 1

Frame 2

Frame 3

Frame 4

10 Paper Boats

Imagination and Travel

OBJECTIVES

In this chapter, we will:

- *read and understand a beautiful poem celebrating a child's love for travel.*
- *understand and appreciate imagery and metaphor.*
- *learn to make a travel brochure.*

WARM-UP

A. What are some of the places you wish to visit on a boat? Name at least three.

1. ....

2. ....

3. ....

B. Now make origami paper boats in different colours. Write the names of places from Exercise A on the boats. Hang the colourful paper boats on a hanger or a stick with strings of different lengths. Hang the mobile hanging in the classroom.

READING

Floating a paper boat is one of the most favourite activities of children. Read this beautiful poem by Rabindranath Tagore to find out what goes on in the mind of a little child who floats his paper boats in a stream.

Day by day I float my paper boats one by one
down the running stream.
In big black letters I write my name on them
and the name of the village where I live.
I hope that someone in some strange land will
find them and know who I am.
I load my little boats with *shiuli* flower from
our garden, and
hope that these blooms of the dawn will be
carried safely to land in the night.
I launch my paper boats and look up into the
sky and see
the little clouds setting their white bulging
sails.
I know not what playmate of mine in the sky
sends them down

the air to race with my boats!
When night comes, I bury my face in
my arms and dream that my
paper boats float on and on under the
midnight stars.
The fairies of sleep are sailing in them,
and the lading is their baskets full of
dreams.

Science Scan

- An object sinks or floats in water depending on how much water it displaces.
- When an object enters water, two forces act upon it. There is a downward force (gravity) and an upward force (buoyancy). Buoyancy is determined by how much water is displaced by the object.
- An object will float if buoyancy is more than gravity. All boats, from the heaviest to the lightest, float on this principle.

running: flowing; moving
stream: a small narrow river
shiuli: white flowers with bright orange stems that blossom in autumn; the official flower of the state of West Bengal
blooms of the dawn: flowers of early morning. (*Shiuli* flowers bloom at night and fall to the ground early in morning)
launch: to put (a boat or ship) into the water
bulging: sticking out in a round shape
lading: goods that are loaded on a ship, boat, etc.

SUMMARY

A small child makes a paper boat, writes his name and that of his village on it, fills it with flowers and floats it in a stream every day. As he floats them, he feels that someone will find them and get to know him. He looks at the sky and imagines that some friend in the sky sends breeze to help his boats sail. When he falls asleep, he dreams that fairies with baskets full of pleasant dreams are sailing on them.

COMPREHENSION

A. Mark the sentences as true (T) or false (F).

1. The poet floats his paper boats in a small puddle. ☐
2. He writes his name and address on the paper boats. ☐
3. He puts red roses in the boats. ☐
4. He thinks that sleep fairies sail in his boats at night. ☐
5. The travellers do not carry anything with them in the paper boats. ☐

B. Read the lines from the poem and answer the questions.

1. *I know not what playmate of mine in the sky*
   sends them down the air to race with my boats!
   a. What does the word *them* refer to here?
   b. Where, according to the poet, is his playmate?
   c. Why does the poet's playmate send them down the air?
2. *The fairies of sleep are sailing in them,*
   and the lading is their baskets full of dreams.
   a. What is meant by the word *lading*?
   b. Who does the poet say is sailing in his paper boats?
   c. What are the travellers carrying with them in the paper boats?

C. Answer the questions.

1. What does the poet write on his paper boats? Why does he do so?
2. Why does the poet put flowers in the paper boats? What is the significance of taking flowers from his own garden?
3. What have the clouds been compared to in the poem?
4. What does the poet do when it is night?
5. The poet creates vivid images in our minds through his words. For example, in the first stanza, we can *see* a little boy floating paper boats in a stream. Describe in your own words an image you like from the poem.
6. If you were in place of the poet, what would you load in the paper boats and why?

Life Skills and Values

Travel and culture

1. Bring a souvenir from a place you have visited or from your hometown. Talk about the item: what it is, what it is meant for/used for, what it is made of, what it represents about the culture of the place etc.
2. Now, discuss the item that fascinated you the most. Which place would you like to visit after having heard about it? What about that place attracted your attention?

VOCABULARY

Metaphor

- A **metaphor** is a figure of speech in which something is referred to as something else to show a similarity.
- The poet calls parts of clouds *bulging sails*. This is a metaphor because the clouds have been compared to sails.
- Read another example: *The baby is a delicate flower.*

  This means the baby is delicate like a flower.

These sentences use metaphors. Underline the two nouns in each sentence that have been compared.

1. Life is a journey to an unknown place.
2. My neighbour thinks life is a fashion show.
3. Shakespeare rightly said that the world is a stage.
4. His mother's soothing words were a balm for him.
5. Our body is a machine that works round the clock.

ACTIVITY

Dolls from different countries

Follow the instructions and make dolls representing different countries in the world.

- Take a strip of slightly stiff paper and fold it in the shape of an accordion. An accordion is a musical instrument. Look it up on the Internet if you haven't seen one.

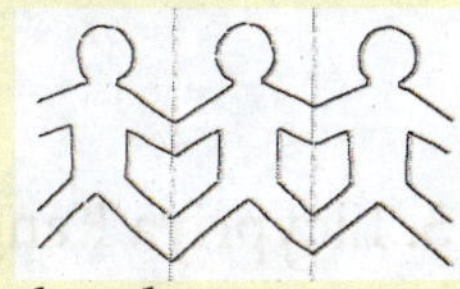

- Draw the template of the paper doll on the top fold.
- Now cut the doll according to the template through all the folds.
- Open the paper cut-out. You will get a chain of dolls appearing to be holding hands.
- Colour the dolls in the colours of the flags of different countries.
- You will get a chain of dolls representing different countries. Put up the doll chain in your classroom.

11 The Happy Prince

Courage in Compassion

OBJECTIVES

In this chapter, we will:

- *read the story of a prince and a swallow.*
- *learn the use of expressions with **do** and **make**.*
- *learn about the active and passive voice.*
- *learn the difference between **whose** and **which**.*
- *listen to a passage and extract information.*
- *interview a character from the story.*
- *learn about the silent letters **k**, **g**, **n**, and **w**.*
- *write a travelogue.*

WARM-UP

It takes a lot of courage to be kind and helpful. Many people in our country have dedicated their lives to helping others. Match the names of these personalities with the work they have done.

1. Kailash Satyarthi	a. A child environmental activist from Manipur trying to create awareness about natural disasters and to reduce their impact
2. Medha Patkar	b. A well-known social activist who has won the Nobel Peace Prize. He has been actively working for children's rights and education and has freed thousands of children from child labour
3. Licypriya Kangujam	c. A famous social activist known for working on issues like social justice for farmers, tribals, Dalits, and people displaced by the construction of the dam along the Narmada River

READING

A statue of a prince observes that some people of his country are suffering. Is he able to help them? Read this adaptation of a story by Oscar Wilde to find out.

High on a column stood the statue of the Happy Prince, **gilded** with gold, two bright **sapphires** for eyes and a large red **ruby** on his sword **hilt**.

He was much admired. 'Why can't you be like the Happy Prince?' asked a mother of her little boy who was crying.

'He looks like an angel,' said the Charity Children.

One night a little Swallow flew over the city. His friends had gone away to Egypt for winter. But he had stayed behind, for he was in love with a **Reed**. 'It is ridiculous,' **twittered** the other Swallows, and flew away.

After they had gone he felt lonely. 'Will you come away with me?' he said to the Reed, but the Reed refused. 'I am off to the **Pyramids**,' the Swallow cried.

All day long he flew, and then he arrived in the city. 'Where shall I put up?'

Then he saw the statue of the Happy Prince. 'I will put up there,' he cried.

He **alighted** between the feet of the Happy Prince and found a golden bedroom. Just as he was going to sleep, a drop of water fell on him. 'How **curious**!' he cried. 'There isn't a single cloud in the sky, yet it is raining.'

Looking Back

- The pyramids of Egypt were built by ancient Egyptians around 4000 years ago as burial places to honour their pharaohs. A pharaoh was a political and religious leader of Egypt.
- There are around 138 Egyptian pyramids. They are all built to the west of the River Nile. The largest is the Great Pyramid of Giza, which is one of the Seven Wonders of the Ancient World.

gilded: covered with a thin layer of gold or gold paint
sapphires: clear, bright blue precious stones
ruby: a dark red precious stone
hilt: the handle (of a sword)
reed: a plant that grows in shallow water
twittered: talked, making short high sounds
pyramids: large buildings with a square or triangular base and sloping sides that meet in a point at the top
alighted: landed after flying
curious: strange and unusual

Another drop fell. He looked up—the Happy Prince was crying.

'Who are you?' the Swallow said.

'I am the Happy Prince.'

'Why are you weeping then?' asked the Swallow.

'When I was alive,' answered the statue, 'I did not cry. My **courtiers** called me the Happy Prince. So I lived, and so I died. Now that I am dead, they have set me up where I can see all the misery of my city. Though my heart is made of **lead**, yet I weep.'

courtiers: persons who are part of the court of a king or queen
lead: a heavy, soft grey metal
poor house: (in former times) an institution in which poor people could live. It was paid for by the public.
seamstress: a woman who sews and makes clothes

'Far away,' continued the statue, 'there is a **poor house**. I can see a **seamstress**. Her face is thin and worn. She is making a gown for the Queen's maids-of-honour. Her boy has fever, and wants oranges. She has only water. Swallow, will you take her my ruby?'

'I'd rather not,' answered the Swallow. But the Happy Prince looked so sad that the Swallow agreed. 'It is very cold here,' he said, 'but I will stay for one night.'

The Swallow plucked the ruby, and flew away with it. At last he came to the poor house. The boy was tossing on his bed, and the mother was asleep. He laid the great ruby on the table and flew back.

'It is curious,' he remarked, 'but I feel quite warm now, although it is so cold.'

'That is because you have done a good deed,' said the Prince.

When day broke, he flew to the river and had a bath.

'To-night I go to Egypt,' said the Swallow.

'Swallow,' said the Prince, 'will you stay one night longer?'

'I am waited for in Egypt,' answered the Swallow.

'I can see a young man,' said the Prince. 'He is trying to finish a play for the Director of the Theatre, but he is too cold and hungry to write. My eyes are made of sapphires. Pluck out one of them and take it to him.'

'Dear Prince,' said the Swallow, 'I cannot do that,' and began to weep.

'Little Swallow,' said the Prince, 'do as I say.'

The Swallow plucked out the Prince's eye. He went and put the sapphire on the table without the student seeing him. When the student looked up, he found the sapphire. 'This is from some great admirer,' he cried. 'Now I can finish my play.'

'I come to say good-bye,' said the Swallow the next day.

'Swallow,' said the Prince, 'will you stay one night longer?'

'It is winter,' answered the Swallow.

'In the **square** below,' said the Happy Prince, 'there stands a little match-girl. Her matches have got spoiled. Her father will beat her if she does not bring some money. Give her my other eye.'

'I will stay with you,' said the Swallow, 'but I cannot pluck out your eye.'

Science Scan

- The seasonal movement of a group of animals from one region to another is called migration.
- Some birds migrate over thousands of kilometres for food or more comfortable weather.
- The Arctic tern has the longest migration of any bird in the world.
- British swallows spend their winters in South Africa.

square: an open area in a town, usually with four sides, surrounded by buildings

'Do as I say,' said the Prince.

The Swallow plucked out the Prince's other eye. He swooped past the match-girl, and slipped the jewel into her hand. 'What a lovely bit of glass!' cried the girl. She ran home, laughing.

'You are blind now,' the Swallow said, 'I will stay with you always.'

'No, little Swallow,' said the Prince, 'you must go to Egypt.'

'I will stay with you,' said the Swallow. All the next day he sat on the Prince's shoulder, and told him stories.

'Swallow,' said the Prince, 'you tell me wonderful stories, but I want to know of the suffering of men. Fly over my city, and tell me what you see.'

swooped: flew downwards, quickly and suddenly
making merry: enjoying oneself
starving: suffering or dying because of a lack of food to eat
leaf: (here) a very thin sheet of metal

The Swallow flew over the city, and saw the rich making merry, while the beggars were sitting in the cold. He saw the white faces of starving children. Under a bridge, two little boys were lying in one another's arms to keep themselves warm. He flew back and told the Prince what he had seen.

'I am covered with gold. You must take it off, and give it to my poor.'

The Swallow picked off the gold, leaf by leaf, till the Happy Prince looked dull and grey.

Then the snow came. The poor Swallow grew colder, but he would not go. He tried to keep himself warm by flapping his wings.

But at last he knew that he was going to die. He flew to the Prince's shoulder. 'Good-bye, dear Prince!' he murmured.

'I am glad that you are going to Egypt,' said the Prince.

'It is not to Egypt that I am going,' said the Swallow. 'I am going to the House of Death.'

He kissed the Happy Prince, and fell dead. A loud crack sounded inside the statue, as if something had broken. The leaden heart had snapped into two.

The next morning the Mayor was walking by. As he passed, he looked up: 'How shabby the Happy Prince looks!' he said. 'And there's a dead bird at his feet!'

'He is no longer beautiful or useful,' said the Art Professor. So, they pulled down the statue and melted it.

'How strange!' said the overseer. 'This broken lead heart will not melt. We must throw it away.' They threw it on a dustheap where the dead Swallow was lying.

'Bring me the two most precious things in the city,' said God to His Angel; the Angel brought Him the leaden heart and the dead bird.

'You have rightly chosen,' said God, 'for in my garden of Paradise, this little bird shall sing for evermore, and in my city of gold the Happy Prince shall praise me.'

snapped: broke suddenly with a sharp noise
Mayor: the head of the government of a town or city, elected by the public
shabby: (looking) old and in bad condition
dustheap: a pile of waste or discarded material
precious: rare and worth a lot of money
Paradise: a perfect place where people are said to go when they die

SUMMARY

Once there was a statue of a prince called the Happy Prince. It was covered with gold, having sapphires for eyes and a ruby in his sword. The Happy Prince could see all the misery of his city but was unable to help anybody. One day, a little swallow landed on the statue. The Happy Prince told the kind Swallow about the sufferings of the people in his city. He requested the Swallow to take the ruby to the poor seamstress, a sapphire to the hungry playwright, and another sapphire to the crying match-girl. When the Prince turned blind, the Swallow decided to stay with the Prince forever and help the poor by picking the gold leaf off the statue, one by one. When the snow came, the poor Swallow could not survive and died. At that moment, the leaden heart of the statue broke into two. Next morning, the dull and grey statue of the Happy Prince was pulled down and melted. But the leaden heart remained intact. It was thrown on a dustheap where the dead Swallow was laid.

COMPREHENSION

A. Fill in the blanks to complete the sentences.

1. The statue of the Happy Prince was covered with ....
2. It had two bright .... for eyes and a large red ....on his sword hilt.
3. The Swallow's friends had gone to .... for winter.
4. The little Swallow stayed back as he was in love with a ....
5. The little Swallow decided to stay at the feet of the .... when he reached the city.

B. Choose the correct option.

1. Though it was winter, the Swallow felt quite warm as
   a. the weather had changed.
   b. the good deed he had done gave him a warm feeling.
   c. he lay at the feet of the Happy Prince.
2. The Swallow decided to stay with the Happy Prince as
   a. he wanted to help the Happy Prince who had become blind.
   b. he began to like the city very much.
   c. it had become warm in Egypt.
3. When the Swallow flew over the city, he saw that
   a. the city had many beautiful skyscrapers.
   b. there was no poverty and suffering in the city.
   c. the poor suffered terribly while the rich enjoyed themselves.

C. Read the sentences from the story and answer the questions.

1. '*Why are you weeping then?*'
   a. Who asks this question and to whom?
   b. Why is the speaker surprised?
2. *A loud crack sounded inside the statue, as if something had broken.*
   a. What had broken inside the statue?
   b. Why did it break?
3. '*Bring me the two most precious things in the city.*'
   a. Who said this and to whom?
   b. What were the two most precious things brought?

D. Answer the questions.

1. Why was the Happy Prince crying?
2. Why did the Happy Prince want to give the ruby to the seamstress?
3. To whom did the Happy Prince send a sapphire from his eye? Why?
4. What impression do you form of the Happy Prince?
5. Do you think that the Swallow was a true friend? Give two reasons to support your answer.

6. If you were the little match-girl, how would you have felt on receiving 'a lovely bit of glass'? How do you think your father would have reacted?

Life Skills and Values

Compassion and patriotism

1. The Happy Prince and the little Swallow display both courage and compassion. Do you agree? Discuss.
2. What qualities should the leader of a country possess? What can she/he do for the people of the country? Share your thoughts.

VOCABULARY

Expressions with *do* and *make*

- *Do* is used to
  - talk about work or tasks.

    I have done the household chores.
  - talk about activities in general.

    Please let me know if I can do something for you.
- *Make* is used to
  - create or build something new.

    She made a boat for herself.
  - indicate the materials that have been used to make something.

    My earrings are made of silver.

A. Underline the correct verb in each sentence.

1. They have all gone to *make/do* shopping.
2. A famous sculptor *made/did* the statue of the Prince.
3. The Prince *did/made* his best to help the poor people in the city.
4. The seamstress had to *make/do* a dress for the Queen's maids-of-honour.
5. The Swallow felt warm because he had *made/done* a good deed.

B. Match the sentence parts in the two columns.

Column A	Column B
1. We must do	a. which woke me up.
2. The bird made a loud sound	b. our duties sincerely.
3. The art professor made a point	c. for the statue to be removed.
4. The mayor made arrangements	d. which made him sleepy in the day.
5. The playwright did his work at night	e. when he said that the statue was no longer beautiful.

GRAMMAR

Active and passive voice

- When the subject of a sentence performs the action, the sentence is said to be in the **active voice**. For example:

  The Swallow plucked the ruby.

  Here, *the Swallow* is the subject and *plucked* is the verb. The subject performed the action of plucking.
- When the subject of a sentence receives the action, the sentence is said to be in the **passive voice**. For example:

  The ruby was plucked by the Swallow.

  The ruby is the subject and it was plucked. The subject receives the action here, so the sentence is in the passive voice.
- In the simple tenses, the form of the verb in the passive voice is:

  the correct form of the verb **be** (*am/is/are/was/were/will be*) + the **past participle of the verb.** For example:

  The student found the sapphire. (active voice)

  The sapphire was found by the student. (passive voice)

  They will write letters. (active voice)

  Letters will be written by them. (passive voice)

A. Read the sentences. Write *A* if the sentence is in the active voice and *P* if it is in the passive voice.

1. The match-girl was scolded by her father. ☐
2. My courtiers called me the Happy Prince. ☐
3. The Swallow laid the great ruby on the table. ☐
4. The little bird sang a sweet song in praise of God. ☐
5. The leaden heart was thrown away by the workers. ☐

Whose and *which*

- *Whose* and *which* can both be used to ask questions.
- They can be used as both pronouns and adjectives.
- *Whose* is used to ask questions about someone or something that belongs to someone else. *Whose* is the possessive form of *who*. For example:

  Whose is this? (used as a pronoun)

  Whose umbrella is this? (used as an adjective)
- *Which* is used to ask questions when there are two or more possible answers or alternatives. For example:

  Which is your cabin? (used as a pronoun)

  Which month has 28 days? (used as an adjective)

B. Fill in each blank with *whose* or *which*.

1. .... birthday is it today?
2. .... house is yours?
3. .... younger brother is he?
4. .... is your favourite season?
5. .... author's book sold a million copies?
6. .... country was hit by an earthquake yesterday?
7. Look at these paintings made by my brother. .... painting do you like the most?

LISTENING AND SPEAKING

Listening

A. Listen to the descriptions of four animals. Make notes while you listen. Then complete the table.

Name	Species	Habitat	Diet category	Fearless trait
Hummingbird		The Americas		
	The rat family			
			Omnivores	
				Can attack large animals like bears and wolves

Speaking

21st CENTURY SKILLS Communication

B. Work in pairs. Imagine you are a television/newspaper reporter who has been asked to interview any one of the characters in the story 'The Happy Prince'. Ask your partner relevant questions. Next, reverse roles and continue the interview.

Here are some examples of questions to ask:

- What role does your character play in the story?
- Why did your character behave in the way it did?
- Would you have acted differently in the situation?

Remember to be polite while asking questions.

Pronunciation

Silent letters *g*, *k*, *n*, and *w*

- There are many silent letters in English, which makes the pronunciation of words quite difficult.
- The letter **g** is often silent when it comes before *n* at the beginning or end of a word. For example: *foreign gnome reign sign*
- The letter **k** is silent when it comes before *n* at the beginning of a word. For example: *knife know knowledge*
- The letter **n** is silent when it comes after *m* at the end of a word. For example: *column hymn solemn*
- The letter **w** is silent at the beginning of a word when it is followed by the letter *r*. For example: *wrap wring write*

C. Read the clues to identify words with a silent letter. Circle the silent letters in the words. One is done for you.

1. It can be difficult to untie. (k)not
2. This is the opposite of *right*. ....
3. You cut vegetables with it. ....
4. This is another word for *pattern*. ....
5. It's a country other than your own. ....
6. This season comes just before winter. ....
7. The meaning of this word is *to leave one's job*. ....
8. This part of the body comes between the hand and the arm. ....

WRITING

Writing a travelogue

- A travelogue is a piece of writing about travels or places visited.
- It gives us detailed information about the attractions of a place.
- To write a travelogue, you must first organise your ideas on the following lines:
  - Location of the place and how it is to be reached
  - Description of the place
  - Cultural or historical background
  - Tourist attractions there
  - Some dos and don'ts to be followed
  - Your own experiences

Recall your most recent trip to a place and write a travelogue. Follow the guidelines given above.

PROJECT 3

Famous LANDMARKS

Can you identify the following statues?

Work in groups of four.

Collect information about any one of these famous statues. Make a travel brochure for the city the statue is famous for. Follow these steps.

- Take two blank sheets of paper and number the pages 1, 2, 3, 4.
- On the cover (first) page, write a catchy title and paste or draw a colourful picture of the statue or other famous monuments of that city.
- On page 2, write a few lines about the history of the city.
- On page 3, write a few interesting facts about the monuments, and paste or draw a few small pictures.
- On page 4, give information about how to reach the monuments.
- Your travel brochure is ready!

12 Dressing Up for Space

Space

OBJECTIVES

In this chapter, we will:

- *study an interesting article on spacesuits.*
- *learn about the etymology of words.*
- *learn about the kinds and transformation of sentences.*
- *learn about if clauses.*
- *listen to a space story and arrange sentences.*
- *enact a short skit on a UFO, or describe a lunar eclipse.*
- *write a short story based on pictures.*

WARM-UP

Mindfulness Activity
Heartbeat exercise

A. All of you must stand up for this activity. Pindrop silence and begin.

- Do jumping jacks for one minute.
- At the end of that minute, place your hand on your heart and pay attention to how your heartbeat and breathing feels.

B. Let's think of dressing up. Pair up with a classmate. Discuss:

- Do we wear the same clothes to school and to party? Why?
- What kind of clothes do you wear at home?
- Imagine your favourite dress. Describe it to your partner.
    - What is it? Jeans and top? Or shorts and T-shirt? A pretty frock?
    - What colour is it? Is it also your favourite colour?
    - Which material is it made of? Is it rough to touch or smooth?
    - Where do you wear it—at home or to party?

C. Have you ever seen the night sky? It is filled with many celestial bodies such as stars, moons, and planets. How many celestial bodies do you know about? Work in pairs and match the name of each celestial body with its description.

Celestial body	Description
1. asteroid 	a. a piece of rock or metal from outer space that has fallen to the earth's surface
2. comet 	b. a celestial object made up of ice and dust that moves around the sun and looks like a bright star with a tail
3. meteor 	c. an artificial body placed in orbit around the earth or moon or another planet to collect information or for communication
4. meteorite 	d. a small rocky body orbiting the sun; large numbers of these, ranging enormously in size, are found between the orbits of Mars and Jupiter
5. satellite 	e. a small body of matter from outer space that burns up when entering the earth's atmosphere and appears as a streak of light in the night sky

READING

Outer space has very harsh conditions. Let's find out what astronauts wear to keep themselves safe in outer space.

Space is, no doubt, a difficult place to travel to and even more difficult to live in. First, there is no air in space. Then it is very cold, unless the sun is shining directly at you. And since there is no air to protect you, the rays of the sun can burn you!

To survive in space, a special spacesuit is needed to protect your body from the effects of the extreme heat and cold, and to provide you with air so that you can breathe. Spacesuits are full of air to provide the pressure that your body is used to on earth. So, they look bloated. Spacesuits also protect you from space dust which travels faster than a bullet!

The special gold-lined visors protect your eyes from bright sunlight. A spacesuit is a complete astronaut protection unit, a very intricate and well-designed machine. It has a heating and cooling system and arrangements for air and water to drink on the go. It even allows the astronaut to relieve himself while in the suit!

The invention of spacesuits

Spacesuits were invented around the 1930s. As one goes higher up in the atmosphere, the air becomes thinner and pilots need air to breathe. In the beginning, the suits were somewhat clumsy as they were quite stiff, bulky, and difficult to move around in.

spacesuit: a special suit worn by astronauts in space
bloated: full of liquid or gas and larger than normal
visors: a pair of transparent, movable shields attached to a helmet to protect the eyes or face
intricate: detailed and complicated
relieve oneself: to urinate or pass stool
bulky: large and heavy

Newer spacesuits for EVA

The earliest astronauts stayed inside their spacecraft but scientists soon realised that the astronauts would also be working in space and so they started working on better spacesuits for these missions.

The first spacesuits were silver in colour because scientists at that time felt that this would reflect the sunrays. They had pipes in them that supplied air and water to keep the astronauts cool.

Soon space missions required extravehicular activity (EVA) on the part of the astronauts. That means the astronauts had to move out of the spacecraft to walk on the moon and, later, to repair the space shuttles while they are in orbit around the earth. The suits had to be changed. They were attached to the spacecraft by a thick tube that carried air and water, and stopped them from floating away.

During Apollo missions, the spacesuits were modified further. They were big backpacks with air, water, and batteries so that the astronauts could do a moonwalk for about eight hours. The thick tubes were removed. The astronauts had more freedom to move around.

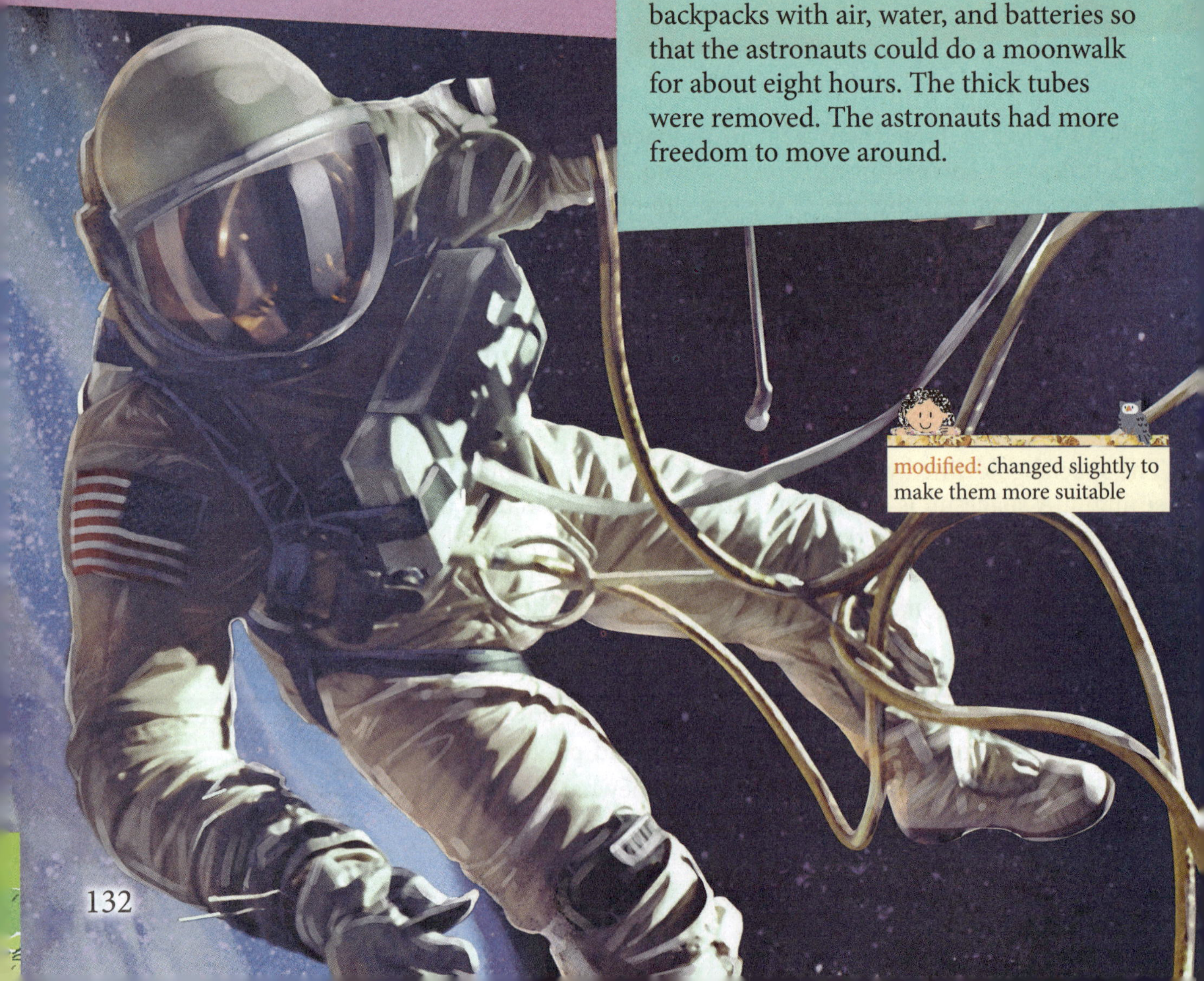

modified: changed slightly to make them more suitable

Flying in SPACE

A spacesuit attached to a rocket-powered backpack is called a manned maneuvering unit (MMU). It has rocket motors to help the astronaut to 'fly' around in space. There is a camera in the astronaut's helmet, so the other crew members and scientists on earth can monitor what the astronaut is doing.

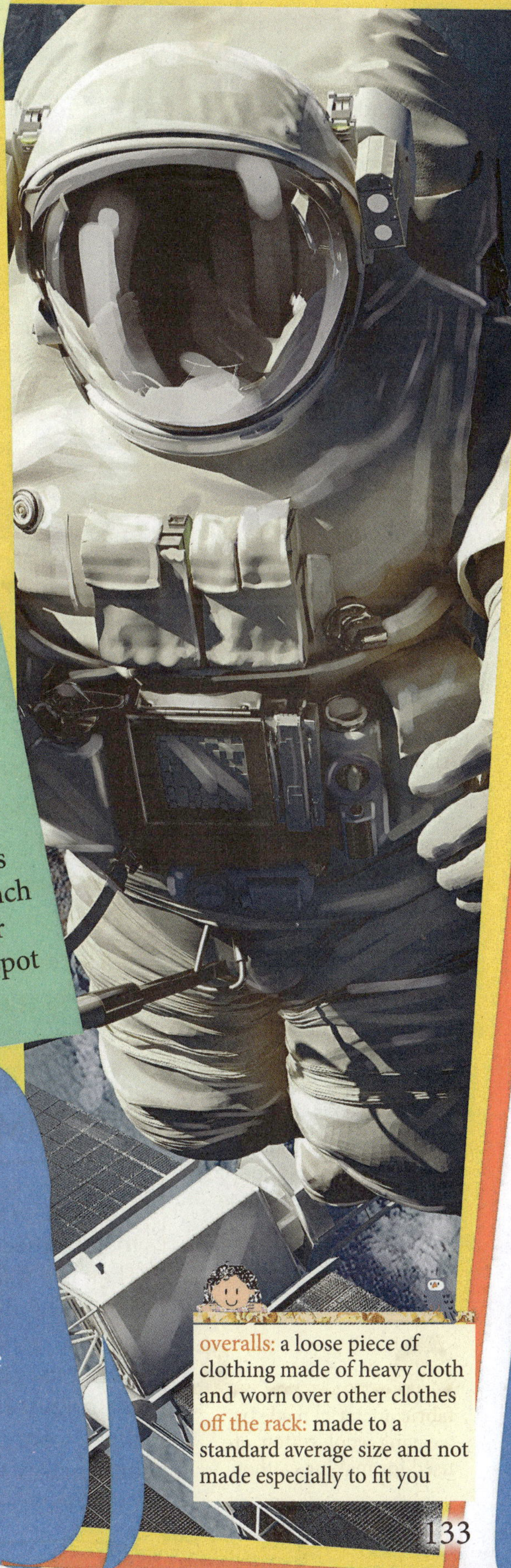

Modern-day spacesuits

Modern-day astronauts don't need to wear spacesuits at all, most of the time. When they are inside a spacecraft, they wear overalls, or even their own clothes. They wear special white spacesuits only when they need to go out into space to do repair work or perform experiments.

The most commonly used spacesuit these days is the orange spacesuit. It is worn only during launch and re-entry. The suit has a parachute and other survival items. It is orange to make it easier to spot the crew.

Interesting facts

Initially, spacesuits were made to fit each astronaut but now they are off the rack—readymade! They are made up of different parts in many sizes that can be attached and will fit astronauts of different sizes. Astronauts can select a suit, pack their bags, and go!

overalls: a loose piece of clothing made of heavy cloth and worn over other clothes
off the rack: made to a standard average size and not made especially to fit you

Fact File

- National Aeronautics and Space Administration (NASA) is an American agency that works on space research projects.
- Apollo 11 was NASA's first space mission to land on the moon, and astronaut Neil Armstrong was the first human to step on the moon. On landing on the moon, Armstrong said, 'That's one small step for (a) man, one giant leap for mankind.'
- Indian Space Research Organisation (ISRO), headquartered in Bengaluru, is the Indian agency that works on space exploration projects.
- Other than successfully launching satellites into orbits, ISRO has also launched *Mangalyaan* and *Chandrayaan* missions to Mars and the moon, respectively.

Spacesuits have eleven layers. The layers are sewn and cemented together. They are about four inches thick. It takes almost two-and-a-half years to produce a suit and it costs around two million dollars.

The spacesuit is too heavy for training on earth. The astronauts use special lightweight parts on earth and they do a lot of training in water. In the pool, they do all the things they will do on their mission.

A spacesuit is not easy to put on. It takes an astronaut over an hour to wear a spacesuit, with the help of an assistant.

Under their helmets, astronauts wear a hat called a Snoopy cap. It has a microphone and speakers, so astronauts can talk to each other. Under the spacesuit, astronauts wear another light suit. It covers their entire body except their head, hands, and feet. There are water tubes in this layer to keep the astronaut cool.

Future spacesuits

In the future, you might be able to go into space for a holiday! Scientists are researching to design spacesuits that will be smaller, lighter, and more comfortable. These suits will be better fitted and made of fabric, with less metal and rubber. Movement in the spacecraft will be easier.

Science Scan

- We cannot hear in space because there is no medium there for sound waves to travel.
- It takes an average of eight minutes and twenty seconds for the light of the sun to reach Earth.

fabric: material made by weaving wool, cotton, etc. used for making clothes

SUMMARY

It can be extraordinarily cold or extremely hot in space due to the absence of air. To survive in space, special suits are a must. They are full of air, protect astronauts from space dust, and have a heating and cooling system with arrangements to provide drinking water. Invented in the 1930s, the spacesuits were bulky and stiff at first. As space science advanced, astronauts needed to venture out in space. It was then that thick pipes were attached to the suits to keep them connected to the spacecraft. However it doesn't end here, and more and more modifications are being added to the spacesuits till today.

COMPREHENSION

A. Fill in the blanks with words from the article.

1. A spacesuit is a complete ....
2. Spacesuits were invented around the ....
3. Spacesuits are filled with air, so they look ....
4. There is no .... to protect you from the sun in space.
5. Spacesuits protect the astronauts from both .... and cold.

B. Choose the correct option.

1. The first spacesuits were silver in colour because
   a. silver shines in the dark.
   b. scientists liked this colour.
   c. scientists thought this colour would reflect the burning hot sunrays.
2. Earlier spacesuits had long pipes attached to them which
   a. supplied air to breathe.
   b. supplied cool water to the suits.
   c. stopped the astronauts from floating away in space.
3. Nowadays, when the astronauts are travelling in a spacecraft,
   a. they wear metal suits.
   b. they wear rubber suits.
   c. they wear overalls or their own clothes.

C. Match the sentence parts in the two columns.

Column A	Column B
1. The orange spacesuit is worn	a. by training in a big pool.
2. The Snoopy cap worn under the helmet	b. only during launch and re-entry.
3. Astronauts take over an hour to put on a spacesuit,	c. is called a manned maneuvering unit.
4. A spacesuit attached to a rocket-powered backpack	d. and they need a helper to put on all the different parts.
5. Astronauts learn how to move around in space in their spacesuits	e. has a radio microphone and speakers so that astronauts can talk to each other.

D. Answer the questions.

1. Describe the earliest spacesuits.
2. What does EVA mean?
3. Why did spacesuits need to be modified during Apollo missions?

4. How do modern spacesuits fit everybody?
5. Why are spacesuits bright orange in colour?
6. How much time and money are needed to make a spacesuit?
7. Do you think in the future everyone will be able to travel to space for a holiday? Give reasons to support your answer.

Life Skills and Values — Exploration and endurance

1. Space is beautiful and fascinating. There is so much to explore about it. There are also dangers because a lot is still unknown. Knowing this, should we still send people into space? Share your thoughts.
2. It is important for astronauts to keep improving their strength and endurance. Talk about one aspect of your life where you need to develop endurance.

VOCABULARY

Etymology

- **Etymology** is the study of the origin of words and their development over the years.
- Many words of the English language come from other languages such as Greek, French, Spanish, and Hindi.
- They are sometimes known as loan words.
- Several of these words are now so common in English that they are considered an essential part of English vocabulary. For example:

Word	Origin
sepoy	Hindi
school	Greek
perfume	French
tomato	Spanish

- Some dictionaries mention the origin of a word that has been borrowed from another language.

Write the name of the language (Greek, Hindi, French, Spanish) from which the following words have been borrowed. You can use the Internet for help.

1. alligator ....
2. ballet ....
3. charpoy ....
4. coat ....
5. croissant ....
6. guru ....
7. mania ....
8. plaza ....
9. shampoo ....
10. war ....

GRAMMAR

Kinds of sentences

There are four kinds of sentences.

- An **declarative sentence** makes a statement of fact. A full stop is put at the end of a declarative sentence. For example:

  Space is a very difficult place to explore.

- An **interrogative sentence** asks a question. A question mark is put at the end of an interrogative sentence. For example:

  Is space a difficult place to explore?

- An **imperative sentence** makes a request or an order. A full stop is put at the end of an imperative sentence. For example:

  Please come with me.

- An **exclamatory sentence** expresses a sudden and strong feeling. An exclamation mark is put at the end of an exclamatory sentence. For example:

  What a difficult place to explore space is!

A. Read these sentences and write *D* for declarative, *In* for interrogative, *Im* for imperative and *E* for exclamatory sentences.

1. Do you wish you could travel in space? ☐
2. A spacesuit weighs approximately 280 pounds. ☐
3. Please take me with you when you go on a holiday. ☐
4. India is making great progress in space technology. ☐
5. How exciting it must have been for Neil Armstrong to be the first man on the moon! ☐

Transformation of sentences

- Read the example sentences on the previous page. Notice the changes made when sentences are transformed from one kind to another.
- Note that:
  - a declarative sentence starts with the subject.
  - an interrogative sentence starts with a question word like *what, who*, etc. or with a helping verb like *does, is*, etc.
  - an imperative sentence starts with the base form of a verb or with *please*, etc. followed by the base form of the verb.

B. Change the following sentences as directed. One is done for you.

1. She is fascinated by space and galaxies.
   (*Change into an interrogative sentence.*)
   Is she fascinated by space and galaxies?
2. Apollo 11 was the first manned spacecraft to land on the moon.
   (*Change into an interrogative sentence.*)
   ....
3. Would you like to have lunch with an astronaut?
   (*Change into a declarative sentence.*)
   ....
4. What an unusual place the moon is!
   (*Change into a declarative sentence.*)
   ....
5. Man has landed on the moon.
   (*Change into an interrogative sentence.*)
   ....

If clauses

- An **if clause** is a clause that expresses a condition.
- It is part of a longer sentence. For example:

  If an astronaut wears a spacesuit, the rays of the sun will not burn him.

The first part of the sentence is an *if* clause.

It uses *If + the simple present tense.*

The second part of the sentence uses the future tense.

So, wearing a spacesuit will make sure that the astronaut is protected from the heat.

- We use sentences with an *if* clause and the simple future to show that the action in the 'if' part of the sentence will result in the action in the other part of the sentence. For example:

  If I meet an astronaut from NASA, I will take his autograph.
  If I work hard, I will be able to fulfil my dream of becoming an astronaut.
- *If clauses* are also called conditional clauses.
- They specify a condition on which the action of the other clause is dependent.

C. Put the verbs in brackets in the correct tense.

1. If I .... (*go*) for a walk, I .... (*take*) you along.
2. If I .... (*see*) him, I .... (*give*) him your number.
3. If he .... (*come*) back early, he .... (*cook*) for himself.
4. If she .... (*want*) to become an astronaut, she .... (*study*) science.

D. Match the sentence parts in the two columns.

Column A	Column B
1. If I visit NASA,	a. I will visit Mars.
2. If I send an email,	b. I shall write an email to NASA.
3. If I enroll to be an astronaut,	c. I may be invited to visit NASA.
4. If I learn to use the computer,	d. I shall enroll to be an astronaut.

LISTENING AND SPEAKING

Listening

A. Listen to the story *My Space Adventure*. Then, read the sentences and number them in the correct order.

1. I ate cookies and pizza. ☐
2. I got inside a rocket and pressed a button. ☐
3. I landed on the moon after I saw a large asteroid. ☐
4. I saw something frightening. It was an alien's spaceship. ☐
5. One of them got out and I asked him: 'What is your name, my alien friend?' ☐
6. Soon, I heard something: 'Sweetheart, it's time to have breakfast!' called Mom. ☐
7. I found my tri-coloured flag. I gave it to him and he went back in his spaceship. ☐
8. He didn't answer; instead he gave me a gift. When I opened it, I saw it was a tiny camera. ☐
9. 'Oh! It was only a dream,' I thought. Even though it was only a dream, it was a great adventure. ☐
10. I put on a spacesuit and a helmet with earphones and speakers, and slept in a sleeping bag with straps. ☐

Speaking

B. Work in groups and do any one of these.

1. **Prepare a short skit on the topic *The Day I Saw a UFO*. Enact the skit in the class.**
2. **Find out what a lunar eclipse is and how it happens. Describe it to a friend as if you are seeing it. Reverse roles.**

21st CENTURY SKILLS Creative Thinking

WRITING

Writing a short story based on pictures

Look at the pictures and write a short story based on them. No picture has been given for the end of the story; end it as you like. Give your story a suitable title.

13 Sailing Out to Space

Space and Curiosity

OBJECTIVES

In this chapter, we will:

- *read a poem about an imaginary ride to space.*
- *study the rhyme scheme of the poem.*
- *make a presentation on a human colony on Mars.*

WARM-UP

Read some fascinating facts about space and space travel.

- The word *astronaut* comes from the Greek words *astron*, which means *star*, and *nautes*, which means *sailor*.
- A space shuttle must start its journey at a minimum speed of nearly 29,000 km per hour, almost nine times faster than a rifle bullet!
- Astronauts report that space smells like hot metal. Some astronauts feel that it smells like a raspberry!
- Astronauts eat dried, frozen food in space. It includes frozen vegetables and desserts, refrigerated food, fruit, etc.
- If one cries in space, the tears don't fall but form bubbles around the eyes because of weightlessness in space.
- We can now use phones and the Internet even in space!

READING

Have you ever dreamt of travelling to space? What would you do in space? Read this poem by Gareth Lancaster to find out what the poet wants to do there.

I dream of sailing out to space[1],
Upon a **yacht** of stars.
With **port holes** all along the sides,
I'd gaze **amazed** at Mars.

With mast **made strong** with spider[2] webs,
And sail of **fluffy** cloud,
I'd watch the Earth go sweeping past,
As out to space I **ploughed**.

With stars in front and stars behind,
And planets far and near,
I'd sail my yacht around the rings,
Of Saturn with a **cheer**.

Science Scan

- Saturn is the second-largest planet in the solar system, but it is very light for its size.
- Saturn has beautiful rings around it, made of billions of tiny chips of ice and dust.

Literary Device

1. and 2. The consonant *s* has been repeated in *sailing out to space* and *strong with spider webs*. Such a repetition of a sound is called **alliteration**.

yacht (pronounced *yawt*): a large sailing boat, often with an engine and a place to sleep on, used for pleasure trips and racing
port holes: small, circular windows on the outside of a ship
amazed: very surprised
made strong: (here) tied together
fluffy: soft and light
ploughed: moved through something
cheer: happiness

And onwards passing Jupiter,
To watch the big, red storm.
Then far around its outer moons,
And through an asteroid swarm.

I dream of sailing out to space[3],
To catch a star or two.
Exploring through the universe,
And just take in the view.

Literary Device

3. The line *I dream of sailing out to space* has been repeated for making a better impact. This is called **repetition**.

Science Scan

- Jupiter, the largest planet in our solar system, is a very stormy planet. One storm, called the Great Red Spot, has lasted over 300 years. This storm is also called the *eye of Jupiter*.
- Jupiter has many moons.

SUMMARY

A young imaginative child makes a big boat of stars, with a mast fastened with spider webs and sails of white clouds. Boarding this boat, the child goes on a trip to space. There he looks at Mars, the spinning Earth, huge stars all around, Saturn and many other planets.

asteroid: any one of the many small planets that go around the sun
swarm: a large group
exploring: travelling around in order to learn about the place
universe: the whole of space and everything in it, including the earth, the planets and the stars

COMPREHENSION

A. Read the lines from the poem and answer the questions.

1. *I'd sail my yacht around the rings...*
   a. Which place is the speaker talking about?
      i. A lake   ii. Space   iii. The sea
   b. What rings does he refer to?
      i. Boxing rings   ii. Rings around Saturn
      iii. Rings worn by a lady on her fingers
2. *I dream of sailing out to space,*
   To catch a star or two.
   a. What is the speaker's dream?
      i. To go on a cruise   ii. To travel to space   iii. To travel around the world
   b. What does he wish to do while fulfilling his dream?
      i. To catch stars   ii. To see wild animals   iii. To visit famous places

B. Answer the questions.

1. What is the yacht in the poet's dream made of?
2. How are the masts fixed to the yacht?
3. What is used to make sails for the yacht?
4. Write a brief description of the poet's journey in space.
5. Draw your own spaceship and describe it. How far would you go in your spaceship?

Life Skills and Values

Imagination

1. Imagination is the basis of all discoveries and inventions. Do you agree? Give reasons to support your answer.
2. Look up the greatest inventions that have changed the world. Which of these fascinate you the most? Why? Which of these have truly changed our lives? Talk about it.

VOCABULARY

Rhyme scheme

- The rhyme scheme is the pattern in which the ends of lines in a poem rhyme.
- To write the rhyme scheme of a poem, we use letters in alphabetical order to show which lines rhyme with each other.
- The end of the first line is marked **a**.
- If the next line rhymes with the line marked **a**, it will also be marked **a**. Otherwise, it will be marked **b**.
- All the rhyming lines are marked with the same letter. For example:

I dream of sailing out to space,	**a**	*Upon a yacht of stars.*	**b**
With port holes all along the sides,	**c**	*I'd gaze amazed at Mars.*	**b**

The words *stars* (second line) and *Mars* (fourth line) rhyme with each other. The rhyme scheme of this stanza is **abcb**.

A. Read the poem and write its rhyme scheme.

Twinkle, twinkle, little star,
How I wonder what you are.
Up above the world so high,
Like a diamond in the sky.
Twinkle, twinkle, little star,
How I wonder what you are!

B. Now write a stanza (four lines) on any topic with the rhyme scheme *abab*.

ACTIVITY

A colony on Mars

Space scientists have been studying the planet Mars for a long time. They are studying the possibility of human beings living on Mars.

Make a scrapbook/PowerPoint presentation/newspaper report titled *Living as Martians*. Include the following information in it with relevant illustrations:

- How far is Mars from Earth?
- Why do scientists think that living on Mars may be possible?
- What problems do you think we may face on Mars?

You may jot down your points below.

Draw what you think a human colony on Mars will look like.

Cross-Curricular Vocabulary

This section lists out all the new words used in the lessons, classified under cross-curricular categories.

Science

Animal world

hind legs: the back legs of an animal

swarm: a large group (of flying insects, such as bees, locusts, and wasps)

Health and safety

bruises: blue, brown or purple marks that appear on the skin after somebody has fallen or been hit

torturing: hurting physically or mentally

Environment

caustic gases: chemical substances that are very powerful and can destroy or dissolve other substances

chopping: cutting into pieces

concrete: building material made by mixing together cement, sand, small stones, and water

emitting: producing or giving out

fumes: smoke, gas, or something similar that smells strongly or is dangerous to breathe in

insecticides: poisonous chemicals used to kill insects

lantana: a small flowering shrub, belonging to America and Africa. Their leaves are poisonous to most animals.

oil crude: (crude oil) oil in its natural state, before it is refined in factories to make petrol and diesel

quarrying: digging out mud from the earth

Natural disasters

famine: extreme scarcity of food

landslides: large amounts of earth and rocks falling down the side of a mountain

rescue: to save (somebody/something) from a dangerous or harmful situation

starving: suffering or dying because of a lack of food to eat

Space

asteroid: any one of the many small planets that go around the sun

port holes: small, circular windows on the outside of a ship or a spacecraft

spacesuit: a special suit worn by astronauts in space

universe: the whole of space and everything in it, including the earth, the planets and the stars

visors: a pair of transparent, movable shields attached to a helmet to protect the eyes or face

Rocks and minerals

emerald: a bright green precious stone

gilded: covered with a thin layer of gold or gold paint

lead: a heavy, soft grey metal

leaf: a very thin sheet of metal

precious: rare and worth a lot of money

ruby: a dark red precious stone

rusted: covered in a reddish-brown substance called rust

sapphires: clear, bright blue precious stones

Social Studies

Our earth

ashore: towards or onto land, having come from an area of water such as the sea or a river

biosphere reserves: places where plants and animals are protected by law passed by the government

island: a piece of land surrounded by water

populous: having many inhabitants

reed: a plant that grows in shallow water

reservoir: an artificial lake formed when a dam is made

seabed: the floor of the sea/ocean

stream: a small narrow river

Heritage and culture

castle: a large strong building with thick high walls and towers, built in the past by kings or queens to defend themselves against attack

palace: the official home of a king, queen or ruler

prayer wheel: A prayer wheel is made of a hollow metal cylinder, and fixed on a handle. On the outside of the cylinder are prayers in Sanskrit. Buddhist devotees spin these wheels.

pyramids: large buildings with a square or triangular base and sloping sides that meet in a point at the top

square: an open area in a town, usually with four sides, surrounded by buildings

throne: a special chair used by a king or queen to sit on during ceremonies

Clothing

fabric: material made by weaving wool, cotton, etc, used for making clothes

overalls: a loose piece of clothing made of heavy cloth and worn over other clothes

robe: a long loose outer piece of clothing, especially one worn as a sign of rank at a special ceremony

Different Parts of Speech

Nouns

agony: great physical or mental pain

avail: help

avarice: greed

broomstick: a broom with a long handle and small thin sticks at the end, or the handle of a broom

courtiers: persons who are part of the court of a king or queen

culprits: persons who have done something wrong or against the law

discontent: not being happy or satisfied

diversity: variety

glare: strong, bright light

hilt: the handle (of a sword)

lading: goods that are loaded on a ship, boat, etc.

Mayor: the head of the government of a town or city, elected by the public

maze: a system of passages designed in a way that it is difficult to find your way through it

Paradise: a perfect place where people are said to go when they die

poor house: (in former times) an institution in which poor people could live; it was paid for by the public

realm: any area of activity, interest, or thought

rungs: the bars that form steps on a ladder

scar: a mark left on your skin after a wound has healed

scarecrow: a figure made to look like a person, that is dressed in old clothes and put in a field to frighten birds away

seamstress: a woman who sews and makes clothes

slumber: deep sleep

solitude: the state of being alone

throng: a crowd of people

trail: way or path

tread: the sound of footsteps

trickster: a person who tricks or cheats people

yacht: a large sailing boat, often with an engine and a place to sleep on, used for pleasure trips and racing

Adjectives

abundant: in large quantities

bloated: full of liquid or gas and larger than normal

churlish: unfriendly, bad-tempered, or rude

curious: strange and unusual

disastrous: disastrous effects cause harm to people or place

endemic: belonging to a particular place

extensive: huge

modified: changed slightly to make something more suitable

motionless: not moving; still

obscure: something difficult to see or to understand

parallel: two lines or objects that are the same distance apart along the whole of their length

perennial: lasting for many years

scandalous: shocking

unaccountable: strange, without any reason

unregulated: not following the law

woebegone: very sad

Adjectives expressing appearances

bulging: sticking out in a round shape

bulky: large and heavy

fluffy: soft and light

gigantic: very big; huge

hideous: extremely ugly or unpleasant

intricate: detailed and complicated

knotted: in knots

mighty: large and impressive

plumper: slightly fatter

shabby: (looking) old and in bad condition

Verbs

accompanied: went with

amazed: very surprised

capture: to catch somebody and keep him/her as a prisoner

ceased: stopped

cheer: happiness

consume: to eat or drink

contradicted: saying what someone has just said is wrong

earned: received something because you deserve it; for example, praise

exploring: travelling around in order to learn about the place

forbade: ordered not to do something

harassing: troubling someone for a long time

intrudes: disturbs

inflicted: made someone experience something unpleasant

obtain: to get something by making an effort

poaching: hunting animals without permission

pretending: behaving in a particular way to make others believe something that is not true

rejoicing: feeling happy about something

restoring: getting something back to its original state

reversed: changed

slipping: coming to an end

smothering: hiding

spots: sees or notices, especially suddenly or when it is not easy to do so

sulking: showing your unhappiness by being silent and moody

summon: to order someone to come to you

suspect: to have an idea that something is probably true but without having definite proof

toil: to work very hard

vanish: disappear

Movement verbs

alighted: landed after flying

emerged: came out (of a dark, confined, or hidden place) expelling: throwing out with force

launch: to put (a boat or ship) into the water

padded: walked softly

ploughed: moved through something

running: flowing; moving

swooped: flew downwards, quickly and suddenly

Sound words

snapped: broke suddenly with a sharp noise

snarled: growled

twittered: talked, making short high sounds

Compound words

empty-handed: without getting what you wanted

foul-tasting: having a very unpleasant taste

Feeling words

anxious: nervous about something which may or may not happen

astonishment: a feeling of very great surprise

eagerly: showing a lot of interest or excitement about something

grateful: feeling or showing an appreciation because somebody has done something kind for you or has done as you asked

soothingly: trying to make someone feel better

sympathetic: kind to somebody who is hurt or sad; showing that you understand and care about others' problems

Phrases and idioms

at stake: that can be won or lost, depending on the success of a particular action

blooms of the dawn: flowers of early morning

from afar: from a distance

hearty meal: a large meal making you feel full

held her in high regard: highly respected her

in vain: without any useful result; without success

iron determination: great strength and desire to do something

just price: fair or correct price

making merry: enjoying oneself

of its own accord: without being asked, forced, or helped; by itself

off the rack: made to a standard average size and not made especially to fit you

on their heels: close behind them

out of sight: not visible any more

parting with the day: the end of day or evening time

passed his way: met someone

plain sailing: extremely easy

pressed in on him: moved towards him

relieve oneself: to urinate or pass stool

set out: to start (a journey)

to and fro: (going) from one place to another and back

toiling time: time for working hard

wadded up: rolled into a tight bundle

Words from Other Languages

Hindi

***Bhaloo*:** a Hindi word for *bear*

didi: a word for 'elder sister' in Hindi and several other Indian languages

Bengali

shiuli: white flowers with bright orange stems that blossom in autumn; the official flower of the state of West Bengal *Shiuli* flowers bloom at night and fall to the ground early in morning

Ladhaki

Aba-ley: 'father' in Ladakhi language

Ama-ley: 'mother' in Ladakhi language

amchi: a doctor practicing the Tibetan system of medicine, also called *amchi*

Azhang-ley: a term used with respect for an elderly man in Ladakhi language

gonpa: a Buddhist monastery

gur-gur tea: butter tea that is made in a long cylindrical wooden vessel. The tea is churned with butter, salt, and milk in this vessel. A low *gur-gur* noise is produced during churning.

Julley: a greeting in Ladakhi language, meaning 'hello' and 'goodbye'

Losar: a festival celebrating the Ladakhi or Tibetan New Year. It has its origin in the fifteenth century.

Memey-ley: 'grandfather' in Ladhaki language